Jekka's
AROMATIC HERBS

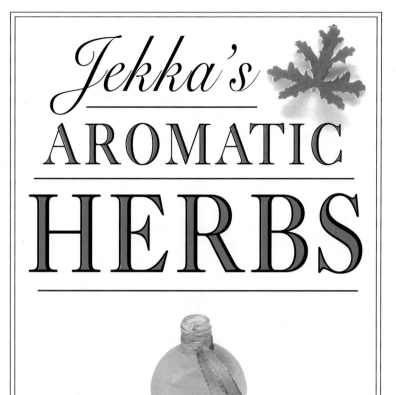

Jekka's AROMATIC HERBS

JEKKA McVICAR

KYLE CATHIE LIMITED

To Hannah

First published as *Jekka's Aromatic Herbs*
in Great Britain in 1995 by
Kyle Cathie Limited
20 Vauxhall Bridge Road, London SW1V 2SA

This edition published 1995

ISBN 1 85626 210 3

2 4 6 8 10 9 7 5 3 1

The material in this book is taken from
Jekka's Complete Herb Book

Photographs © Jessica McVicar 1994
© Michelle Garrett 1994 © Sally Maltby 1994

Artwork © Sally Maltby 1994

Book design by Geoff Hayes
Cover design by Tom Murdoch and Geoff Hayes

Printed and bound in Spain
by Graficas Reunidas, S.A., Madrid

Acknowledgements
With many thanks to Mac for all his support, Anthea for turning up in the nick of time, Kyle for taking the gamble, Piers for all his reading and Penny for her compliments.

Photographic acknowledgements
Plant photography by Jekka McVicar and Sally Maltby.
All other photography by Michelle Garrett.

CONTENTS

Introduction

'Here's flowers for you;
Hot lavender, mints, savory, marjoram,
The marigold, that goes to bed wi' the sun,
And with him rises weeping.'
Shakespeare

Herbs have been used since man has been on Earth as a food and a medicine. There are few plants capable of providing the sheer pleasure of herbs, they are the most generous of plants, aromatic and attractive, useful in both the home and the garden, health-giving and healthy.

The increasing interest in herbs is part of a movement towards a healthier lifestyle, symbolising a more natural approach. Herbs are used in cooking, in domestic products, alternative medicines and cosmetics, and they affect the quality of life in many ways.

The most extraordinary feature of herbs is their incredible versatility. You may think of a particular herb as having mainly culinary or medicinal properties and then discover it has other useful applications. Thyme, for example, provides the raw material for cooking, medicines and aromatherapy.

What is a herb? It can be argued that all useful plants are herbs. The Oxford English Dictionary defines them as 'Plants of which the leaves, stem or flowers are used for food or medicine, or in some way for their scent or flavour'. To elaborate, a herb can be any plant used as an ingredient in food or drink for flavour or preservative properties, in medicine for health-giving properties, or in perfume, cosmetics or aromatherapy as a fixative, for flavour or aroma or as a cleansing agent. That herbs do you good is in no doubt, improving your health, appearance or sense of well-being.

The use of herbs for their aromatic properties dates back in history. The Romans used lavender water to scent their bathing water. During the eras of plague and pestilence people sprinkled themselves with the oil of rosemary, thyme or sage, as these herbs, quite apart from smelling good, have antiseptic qualities which helped to ward off the bugs. In the olden days, before deodorants, people carried nosegays made of lavender, hyssop, thyme and sage to smell as they walked down the polluted streets. Scented geraniums were grown in pots by the Victorians which were then placed along the paths so that when they walked their long dresses brushed against the plants sending up a mixture of scents such as rose, peppermint and nutmeg to name a few.

Now a days scent is very evocative and planting aromatic herbs gives one that heady smell of summer, mixed with the nostalgia of the summer holidays. It is recognised that if something smells good it makes one feel good and I can think of nothing better than brushing past a lavender bush, the aroma alone soothes the spirits, and when it flowers and becomes covered in butterflies it is a sight to gladden the eye. On a summers evening Musk mallow comes into its own, the scent is a warm musky aroma hence its common name. As for the Primrose, it is the first sign of spring and the sweet smell and sunny face certainly lift the spirits and proves that summer is on its way. When planning a herb garden there are no restrictions on how it should be laid out, formally or informally, as a border, or in a pot. The only factors you must consider are: what are the soil conditions like? How sunny or shady is the area you have chosen? Would this suit the herbs you want to plant? If you find the area unsuitable for a particular herb and you have no wish to re-design your garden, plant them in containers as you will find that most herbs are accommodating plants and will grow happily in them as long as you take due consideration of their root size. This then frees you to place them in the position that most suits them and yours design. If necessary sinking the pots into the ground to disguise them. Bearing in mind that this is a aromatic herb garden plant the herbs near the house so the scent wafts in on a summers evening, or along a path so one brushes past as one goes to the door. Remember as well as being aromatic Thyme, Lemon Verbena, Hyssop, Sage, Lavender are all edible, so plant them so they can be used. Finally I must stress that all herbs grown for either culinary or medicinal use should be grown free from the use of chemicals.

Jekka McVicar

PROPAGATION

One of the great joys of gardening is propagating your own plants. Success is dependent on adequate preparation and the care and attention you give during the critical first few weeks. The principles remain the same, but techniques are constantly changing. There is always something new to discover.

The three main methods of propagating new plants are by Seed, Cuttings and Layering.

This chapter provides general, step-by-step instructions for each of these methods. As there are always exceptions to a rule, please refer to the propagation section under each individual herb.

SEED

Sowing Outside
Most annual herbs grow happily propagated year after year from seed sown directly into the garden. There are two herbs worth mentioning where that is not the case – sweet marjoram, because the seed is so small it is better started in a pot; and basil because, in damp northern climates like that in Britain, the young seedlings will rot off.

In an average season the seed should be sown in mid- to late spring after the soil has been prepared and warmed. Use the arrival of weed seedlings in the garden as a sign that the temperature is rising. Herbs will survive in a range of different soils. Most culinary herbs originate from the Mediterranean so their preference is for a sandy free-draining soil. If your soil is sticky clay do not give up, give the seeds a better start by adding a fine layer of horticultural sand along the drill when preparing the seed bed.

Preparation of Seed Bed
Before starting, check your soil type making sure that the soil has sufficient food to maintain a seed bed. Dig the bed over, mark out a straight line with a piece of string secured tightly over each row, draw a shallow drill, 6-13mm (¼/½in) deep, using the side of a fork or hoe, and sow the seeds thinly, 2 or 3 per 25mm (1in). Do not overcrowd the bed, otherwise the seedlings will grow leggy and weak and be prone to disease.

Protected Sowing
Starting off the seeds in a greenhouse or on a windowsill gives you more control over the warmth and moisture they need, and enables you to begin propagating earlier in the season.

Nothing is more uplifting than going into the greenhouse on a cold and gloomy late-winter morning and seeing all the seedlings emerging. It makes one enthusiastic for spring.

Preparation of Seed
Most seeds need air, light, temperature and moisture to germinate. Some have a long dormancy, and some have hard outer coats and need a little help to get going. Here are two techniques.

Scarification
If left to nature, seeds that have a hard outer coat would take a long time to germinate. To speed up the process, rub the seed between 2 sheets of fine sandpaper. This weakens the coat of the seed so that moisture essential for germination can penetrate.

Stratification (vernalization)
Some seeds need a period of cold (from 1 to 6 months) to germinate. Mix the seed with damp sand and place in a plastic bag in the refrigerator or freezer. After 4 weeks sow on the surface of the compost and cover with Perlite. My family always enjoys this time of year. They go to the freezer to get the ice cream and find herb seed instead.

Preparation of Seed Container
One of the chief causes of diseased compost is a dirty propagation container. To minimize the spread of disease, remove any 'tidemarks' of compost, soil chemicals around the inside of the pots and seed trays. Wash and scrub them thoroughly with washing up liquid, rinse with water and give a final rinse with diluted Jeyes fluid. Leave for 24 hours before re-use. Old compost also provides ideal conditions for damping off fungi and sciarid flies. To avoid cross-infection always remove spent compost from the greenhouse or potting shed.

Compost
It is always best to use a sterile seed compost. Ordinary garden soil contains many weed seeds that could easily be confused with the germinating herb seed. The compost used for most seed sowing is 50per cent propagating bark and 50per cent peat-based seed compost and unless stated otherwise within the specific herb section, this is the mix to use. However, for herbs that

Misting Unit

efer a freer draining
mpost, or for those that
quire stratification
atside, I advise using a 25
er cent peat-based seed
mpost: 50 per cent
opagating bark and 25 per
nt horticultural grit mix.
ad if you are sowing seeds
at have a long germination
riod, use a soil-based seed
mpost.

owing in Seed Trays
eparation: fill a clean seed
ay with compost up to 1cm
2in) below the rim and
m down with a flat piece
wood. Do not to press too
ard as this will over-
ompress the compost and
strict drainage, encourag-
g damping off disease and
tack by sciarid fly.
The gap below the rim is
sential, as it prevents the
rface sown seeds and
ompost being washed over
e edge when watering, and
allows room for growth
hen you are growing under
rd or glass.
Water the prepared tray
sing a fine rose on the
atering can. Do not over-
ater. The compost should
e damp, not soaking. After
n initial watering, water as
tle as possible, but never
t the surface dry out. Once
e seed is sown lack of
oisture can prevent
rmination and kill the
edlings, but too much
ater excludes oxygen and
acourages damping-off
ingi and root rot. Be sure
use a fine rose on the
atering can so as not to
sturb the seed.

owing Methods
here are 3 main methods,
ie choice dependent on
ie size of the seed. They
e, in order of seed size,
ne to large:

Scatter on the surface of
ie compost, and cover with
fine layer of Perlite.

Press into the surface of
ie compost, either with
our hand or a flat piece of
ood the size of the tray,

and cover with Perlite.
3 Press down to 1 seed's
depth and cover with
compost.

The Cardboard Trick
When seeds are too small to
handle, you can control
distribution by using a thin
piece of card (cereal cartons
are good), cut to 10cm x
5cm (4in x 2in), and folded
down the middle. Place a
small amount of seed into
the folded card and gently
tap it over the prepared seed
tray. This technique is
especially useful when
sowing into plug trays (see
below).

Sowing in Plug (Module) Trays (Multi-cell Trays)
These plug trays are a great
invention. The seed can
germinate in its own space,
get established into a strong
seedling, and make a good
root ball. When potting on,
the young plant remains
undisturbed and will
continue growing, rather
than coming to a halt
because it has to regenerate
roots to replace those
damaged in pricking out
from the seed tray. This is
very good for plants like
coriander, which hate being
transplanted and tend to
bolt if you move them.
Another advantage is that as
you are sowing into
individual cells, the problem
of overcrowding is cut to a
minimum, and damping-off
disease and sciarid fly are
easier to control. Also,
because seedlings in plugs
are easier to maintain,
planting out or potting on is
not so critical.
Plug trays come in different
sizes; for example, you can
get trays with very small
holes of 15mm (½in) x

15mm up to trays with holes
of 36.5mm (1¼in) x
36.5mm. To enable a
reasonable time lapse
between germination and
potting on, I recommend
the larger.
When preparing these trays
for seed sowing, make sure
you have enough space,
otherwise compost seems to
land up everywhere. Prepare
the compost and fill the tray
right to the top, scraping off
surplus compost with a piece
of wood level with the top of
the holes. It is better not to
firm the compost down.
Watering in (see above)
settles the compost enough
to allow space for the seed
and the top dressing of
Perlite. For the gardener-in-
a-hurry there are available in
good garden centres ready-
prepared propagation trays,
which are plug trays already
filled with compost. All you
have to do is water and add
the seed.
The principles of sowing in
plug trays are the same as
for trays. Having sown your
seed, DO label the trays
clearly with the name of the
plant, and also the date. The
date is useful as one can
check their late or speedy
germination. It is also good
for record keeping, if you
want to sow them again next
year, and helps with
organizing the potting on.

Seed Germination
Seeds need warmth and
moisture to germinate.
The main seed sowing
times are autumn and
spring. This section provides
general information with the
table below providing a
quick look guide to
germination. Any detailed
advice specific to a particular
herb is provided in the A-Z
Herb section.

Quick Germination Guide
Hot 27-32°C (80-90°F)
Rosemary

Warm 15-21°C (60-70°F)
Most plants, including those
from the Mediterranean,
and Chives and Parsley.

Cool 4-10°C (40-50°F)
Lavenders. (Old lavender
seed will need a period of
stratification).

Stratification
Arnica (old seed), Sweet
Woodruff, Yellow Iris,
Poppy, Soapwort, Sweet
Cicely, Hops (old seed),
Sweet Violet.

Scarification
All leguminous species, i.e.,
broom, trefoils, clovers and
vetches.

Need Light (i.e., do not cover)
Chamomile, Foxglove,
Thyme, Winter Savory,
Poppy and Sweet Marjoram.

In a cold greenhouse, a
heated propagator may be
needed in early spring for
herbs that germinate at
warm to hot temperatures.
In the house you can use a
shelf near a radiator (never
on the radiator), or an
airing cupboard. Darkness
does not hinder the
germination of most herbs
(see table above for
exceptions), but if you put
your containers in an airing
cupboard YOU MUST
CHECK THEM EVERY DAY.
As soon as there is any sign
of life, place the trays in a
warm light place, but not in
direct sunlight.

Hardening Off
When large enough to
handle, prick out seed tray
seedlings and pot up
individually. Allow them to
root fully.
Test plug tray seedlings by
giving one or two a gentle
tug. They should come away
from the cells cleanly, with
the root ball. If they do not,
leave for another few days.
When the seedlings are
ready, harden them off
gradually by leaving the
young plants outside during
the day. Once weaned into a
natural climate, either plant
them directly into a
prepared site in the garden,
or into a larger container for
the summer.

CUTTINGS

Taking cuttings is sometimes the only way to propagate (e.g. non-flowering herbs, such as **Chamomile Treneague**, and variegated forms, such as Tri-color Sage).

It is not as difficult as some people suggest, and even now I marvel at how a mere twig can produce roots and start the whole life cycle going again.

There are 4 types of cutting used in herb growing:

1 Softwood cuttings taken in spring

2 Semi-hardwood cuttings taken in summer

3 Hardwood cuttings taken in autumn

4 Root cuttings, which can be taken in spring and autumn.

For successful softwood cuttings it is worth investing in a heated propagator, which can be placed either in a greenhouse or on a shady windowsill. For success-ful semi-ripe, hardwood and root cuttings, a shaded cold frame can be used.

Softwood Cuttings

Softwood cuttings are taken from the new lush green growth of most perennial herbs between spring and mid-summer, a few examples being Balm of Gilead, Bergamot, the Chamomiles, the Mints, Prostanthera, the Rosemarys, the Scented Geraniums, the Thymes, Curly Wood Sage and Wormwood. Check under the individual herb entries in the A-Z section for more specific information.

1 The best way to get a plant to produce successful rooting material is to prune it vigorously in winter (which will encourage rapid growth when the temperature rises in the spring), and to take cuttings as soon as there is sufficient growth.

2 Fill a pot, seed tray, or plug tray with cutting compost – 50 per cent bark, 50 per cent peat. It is important to use a well-draining medium rather than standard potting mixes as, without root systems, cuttings are prone to wet rot.

Firm the compost to within 2cm (¾in) of the rim.

If space is limited or pots are unavailable, you can pack the base of several cuttings in damp sphagnum moss (rolled up firmly in a polythene strip and held in place by a rubber band or string) until the roots form.

3 Collect the cuttings in small batches in the morning. Choose sturdy shoots with plenty of leaves. Best results come from non-flowering shoots with the base leaves removed. Cut the shoot with a knife, not scissors. This is because scissors tend to pinch or seal the end of the cutting thus hindering rooting.

4 Place the cutting at once in the shade in a polythene bag or a bucket of water. Softwood cuttings are extremely susceptible to water loss; even a small loss will hinder root development. If the cuttings cannot be dealt with quickly, keep them in the cool (e.g. in a salad box from a refrigerator) to prevent excessive water loss.

5 To prepare the cutting material, cut the base of the stem 5mm (¼in) below a leaf joint, to leave a cutting of roughly 10cm (4in) long.

6 If the cutting material has to be under 10cm (4in), take the cutting with a heel. Remove the lower leaves and trim the tail which is left from the heel.

7 Trim the stem cleanly before a node, the point at which a leaf stalk joins the stem. Remove the leaves from the bottom third of the cutting, leaving at least 2 or 3 leaves on top. The reason for leaving leaves on cuttings is that the plant feeds through them as it sets root. Do not tear off the base leaves as this can cause disease; use a knife and gently cut them off.

8 Make a hole with a dibber in the compost and insert the cutting up to its leaves. Make sure that the leaves do not touch or go below the surface of the compost; they will rot away and may cause a fungus condition which can spread up the stem and to other cuttings. Do not overcrowd the container or include more than one species, because quite often they take different times to root. (For instance, keep box and thymes separate.)

Hormone rooting-powders that some gardeners use, contain synthetic plant hormones and fungicide and are not for the organic grower; following my detailed instructions you should find them unnecessary. However, they may help with difficult cuttings. The cutting should be dipped into the rooting-powder just before inserting into the compost.

9 Label and date the cuttings clearly, and only water the compost from above if necessary (the initial watering after preparing the container should be sufficient). Keep out of direct sunlight in hot weather. In fact, if it is very sunny, heavy shade is best for the first week.

Either place in a heated or unheated propagator, or cover the pot or container with a plastic bag supported on a thin wire hoop (to prevent the plastic touching the leaves), or with an upturned plastic bottle with the bottom cut off. If you are using a plastic bag, make sure you turn it inside out every few days to stop exc[ess] moisture from condensati[on] dropping onto the cutting[s].

10 Spray the cuttings ever[y] day with water for the first week. Do this in the morning, never at night. I[f] not test for rooting too ea[rly] by tugging the cutting up, you may disturb it at a crucial time. A better way [to] check for new roots is to look underneath the container. Average rootin[g] time is 2-4 weeks.

The cutting medium is lo[w] in nutrients, so give a regular foliar feed when th[e] cutting starts to root.

11 Harden off the cutting[s] gradually when they are rooted. Bring them out in stages to normal sunny, ai[ry] conditions.

12 Pot them on using a prepared potting compost once they are weaned. Lab[el] and water well after transplanting.

13 About 4-5 weeks after transplanting, when you c[an] see that the plant is growi[ng] away, pinch out the top centre of the young cuttin[g]. This will encourage the plant to bush out, making [it] stronger as well as fuller.

14 Allow to grow on until [a] good-size root ball can be seen in the pot – check occasionally by gently removing the plant from t[he] pot – then plant out.

Semi-hardwood Cuttings o[r] Greenwood Cuttings

Usually taken from shrubb[y] herbs such as Rosemary an[d] Myrtle towards the end of the growing season (from mid-summer to mid-autumn). Use the same method (steps 2-8) as for softwood cuttings, with the following exceptions:

2 The compost should be freer-draining than for softwood cuttings, as semi-hardwood cuttings will be left for longer (see 10 elow). Make the mix equal arts peat, grit and bark.

Follow step 9 for softwood uttings, but place the pot, ed tray or plug tray in a old greenhouse, cold ame, cool conservatory, or n a cold windowsill in a arage, not in a propagator, nless it has a misting unit.

0 Average rooting time for emi-hardwood cuttings is 4-weeks. Follow step 10 xcept for the watering chedule. Instead, if the utumn is exceptionally hot nd the compost or cuttings eem to be drying out, spray nce a week. Again, do this n the morning, and be areful not to over-water.

1 Begin the hardening off rocess in the spring after he frosts. Give a foliar feed s soon as there is sufficient ew growth.

Hardwood Cuttings
aken mid- to late autumn n exactly the same way as oftwood cuttings steps 2-8, ut with a freer draining ompost of equal parts peat, rit and bark. Keep watering o the absolute minimum. Vinter in a cold frame, reenhouse or conservatory. Average rooting time can ake as long as 12 months.

Root Cuttings
This method of cutting is uitable for plants with reeping roots, such as ergamot, Comfrey, Horseradish, Lemon Balm, Mint. Soapwort and Sweet Voodruff.

Dig up some healthy roots n spring or autumn.

Fill a pot, seed tray or lug tray with cutting ompost – 50 per cent bark, 0 per cent peat, firmed to vithin 3cm (1in) of the rim. Water well and leave to tand while preparing your utting material.

Cut 4-8cm (1.5-3in) engths of root that carry a

growing bud. It is easy to see the growing buds on the roots of mint.

This method is equally applicable for all the varieties mentioned above as suitable for root propagation, with the exception of Comfrey and Horseradish, where one simply slices the root into sections, 4-8cm (1½-3in) long, using a sharp knife to give a clean cut through the root. Do not worry, each will produce a plant!
   These cuttings lend themselves to being grown in plug trays.

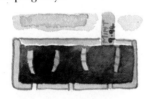

4 Make holes in the compost with a dibber. If using pots or seed trays these should be 3-6cm (1-2½in) apart. Plant the cutting vertically.

5 Cover the container with a small amount of compost, followed by a layer of Perlite level with the top of the container.

6 Label and date. This is most important because you cannot see what is in the container until the plant begins to grow and it is all too easy to forget what you have planted.

7 Average rooting time 2-3 weeks. Do not water until roots or top growth appears. Then apply liquid feed.

8 Slowly harden off the cuttings when rooted.

9 Pot on in a potting

compost once they are weaned. Label and water well after transplanting. You can miss this stage out if you have grown the root cuttings in plug trays.

10 About 2-3 weeks after transplanting, when you can see that the plant is growing away, pinch out the top centre of the young cutting. This will encourage the plant to bush out, making it stronger as well as fuller.

11 Allow to grow on until a good-size root ball can be seen in the pot. Plant out in the garden when the last frosts are over.

LAYERING

If cuttings are difficult to root you can try layering, a process that encourages sections of plant to root while still attached to the parent. Bay, Rosemary, Sage are good examples of plants that suit this method.

1 Prune some low branches off the parent plant during the winter season to induce vigorous growth and cultivate the soil around the plant during winter and early spring by adding peat and grit to it.

2 Trim the leaves and side shoots of a young vigorous stem for 10-60cm (4-24in) below its growing tip.

3 Bring the stem down to ground level and mark its position on the soil. Dig a trench at that point, making one vertical side 10-15cm (4-6in) deep, and the other sloping towards the plant.

4 Roughen the stem at the point where it will touch the ground.

5 Peg it down into the trench against the straight side, then bend the stem at right angles behind the growing tip, so that it protrudes vertically. Then

return the soil to the trench to bury the stem. Firm in well.

6 Water well using a watering can and keep the soil moist, especially in dry periods.

7 Sever the layering stem from its parent plant in autumn if well rooted, and 3-4 weeks later nip out the growing tip from the rooted layer to make plant bush out.

8 Check carefully that the roots have become well established before lifting the layered stem. If necessary, leave for a further year.

9 Replant either in the open ground or in a pot using the bark, grit, peat mix of compost. Label and leave to establish.

Mound Layering
A method similar to layering that not only creates new growth but also improves the appearance of old plants. This is particularly suitable for sages and thymes, which can woody in the centre.

1 In the spring, pile soil mixed with peat and sand over the bare woody centre until only young shoots show.

2 By late summer, roots will have formed on many of these shoots. They can be taken and planted in new locations as cuttings or by root division.

3 The old plant can then be dug up and disposed of.

POTPOURRI GARDEN

Home-made potpourris are warm, not flashy in colour, and the aroma is gentle.

This garden is planted with herbs that can be dried and used in the making of potpourris. The leaves and petals should be harvested, dried and stored as per

Harvesting, There is also further information under the individual species.

Position this garden in full sun to make the oils come to the surface of the leaves and get the benefit of the aroma. Also, as it has turned out to

be a fairly tender garden, the soil will need a little bit of extra attention to ensure that it is very well drained. There are also some herbs that will need lifting in the autumn – lemon verbena, sage pineapple, and the

scented geranium 'Attar of Roses'. Equally, if you live in a damp, cold place, the myrtle and lavender dentata will need protection. When planting, note that I have put the honeysuckle in the corner to give it a wall or fence to climb up.

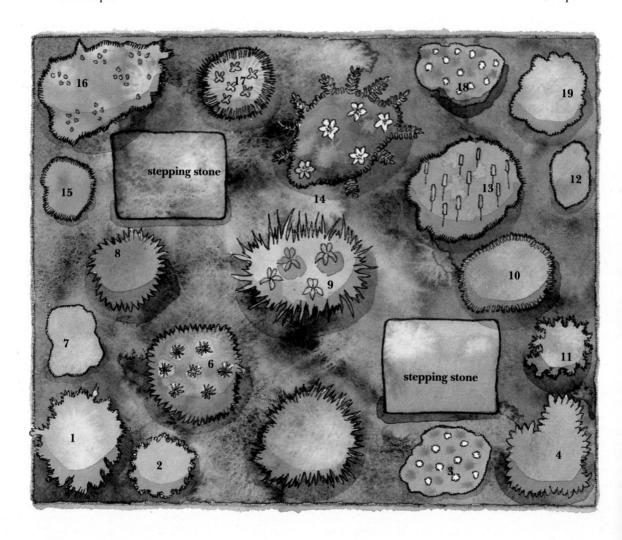

1	**Southernwood** *Artemisia abrotanum*
2+17	**Heliotrope** *Heliotropium arborescens*
3+18	**Chamomile, double flowered** *Chamaemelum nobile* 'Flore Pleno'
4	**Roses, Damask rose** *Rosa damascena*
5	**Lemon Verbana** *Aloysia triphylla*
6	**Bergamot** *Monarda didyma*
7	**Thyme, orange-scented** *Thymus x citriodorus* 'Fragrantissimus'
8	**Sage, Pineapple** *Salvia elegans* 'Scarlet Pineapple'

9	**Orris** *Iris* 'Florentina'
10	**Pinks, Doris** *Dianthus splendens* 'Doris'
11	**Scented Geranium** *Pelargonium* 'Attar of Roses'
12	**Thyme Caraway** *Thymus herba-barona*
13	**Lavender Dentata** *Lavandula dentata*
14	**Myrtle** *Myrtus communis*
15	**Hyssop Rock** *Hyssopus officinalis spp. aristatus*
16	**Rosemary Benenden Blue** *Rosmarinus officinalis* 'Benenden Blue'
19	**Oregano** *Origanum vulgare*

AROMATHERAPY HERB GARDEN

One of the things I enjoy about growing herbs is the scent. Aroma is very evocative, and aromatherapy is growing in importance today. This garden has been designed not to create one's own oils, which is a complex process, but to have those aromas around that help our everyday lives, and to make an attractive garden, as the plants all have useful qualities apart from their aroma. The sweet marjoram, basil, thyme, fennel and rosemary are excellent culinary herbs. The chamomile and lemon balm make good herbal teas to help one relax.

I have placed paving stones in the garden to make access to the plants easier. However, when this garden becomes established, the stones will barely show.

I include a list of the herbs in this garden with the properties of the essential oil.

	Herb	Properties of the Essential Oil
1	**Basil** *Ocimum basilicum*	Concentration
2	**Bergamot** *Monarda fistulosa*	Uplifting
3	**Chamomile** *Chamaemelum nobile*	Relaxing
4	**Fennel** *Foeniculum vulgare*	Antitoxic
5	**Scented Geranium graveolens** *Pelargonium graveolens*	Relaxing
6	**Hyssop** *Hyssopus officinalis*	Sedative
7	**Juniper** *Juniperus communis*	Stimulant
8	**Lemon Balm** *Melissa officinalis*	Anti-depressnat
9	**Lavender** *Lavandula angustifolia*	Soothing
10	**Rosemary** *Rosmarinus officinalis*	Invigorating
11	**Sweet Marjoram** *Origanum majorana*	Calming
12	**Thyme** *Thymus vulgaris*	Stimulant

Cedronella canariensis (triphylla)

BALM OF GILEAD

Also known as Canary Balm. From the family Labiatae

Although this herb originates from Madeira and the Canary Islands, as indicated by its species name, balm of Gilead is now established in many temperate regions of the world. Many plants have been called balm of Gilead, the common link that they all have a musky, eucalyptus, camphor-like scent.

The Queen of Sheba gave Solomon a balm of Gilead, which was *Commiphora opobalsamum*, an aromatic desert shrub found in the Holy Land. Today this plant is rare and protected, its export prohibited.

The balm of Gilead mentioned in the Bible ('Is there no balm in Gilead; is there no physician there?') was initially held to be *Commiphora meccanensis* which was an aromatic shrub. However some now say it was oleo-resin obtained from *Balsamodendron opobalsamum*, a plant now thought to be extinct. Whatever is the case, the medicinal balm of Gilead is *Populus balsamifera*. This is balsam poplar, a tree found growing in several temperate countries, which smells heavenly in early summer, while the herb now known as balm of Gilead is *Cedronella canariensis*. This is said to have a similar scent to the Biblical shrubs, perhaps the reason for its popular name.

Balsam poplar *Populus balsamifera*

SPECIES

Cedronella canariensis (triphylla)
Balm of Gilead
Half-hardy perennial, partial evergreen. Ht 1m (3ft), spread 60cm (2ft). Leaves with strong eucalyptus scent, 3 lobes and toothed edges, borne on square stems. Pink or pale mauve, two-lipped flowers throughout summer. Black seed heads.

CULTIVATION

Propagation
Seed
The fairly small seeds should be sown directly on the surface of a prepared pot, plug or seed tray. Cover with a layer of Perlite.

It is a temperamental germinator so bottom heat of 20°C (68°F) can be an asset. If using heat remember not to let the compost dry out, and only water with a fine spray when needed. The seedlings will appear any time between 2–3 weeks. When 2 leaves have formed, prick out and plant in position 1m (3ft) apart.

Cuttings
More reliable than seed. They take readily either in early summer before flowering on new growth or in early autumn on the semi-ripe wood. Use the bark, peat, grit mix of compost (see Propagation).

Pests and Diseases
Being aromatic, aphids and other pests usually leave it alone, but the seedlings are prone to damping off.

Maintenance
Spring: Sow seeds under protection. In a warm garden a mature plant can self-seed; rub the leaves of any self-seedlings to see if it is balm of Gilead or a young nettle (but don't get stung!). At this stage their aroma is the only characteristic which tells them apart.
Plants over-wintered in containers should be repotted if root-bound and given a liquid feed.
Summer: Cut back after flowering to keep it neat and tidy, and also to encourage new growth from which late cuttings can be taken.
Autumn: Take stem cuttings. Collect seed heads.
Winter: Protect from frost.

Balm of Gilead
Cedronella canariensis

Garden Cultivation
Balm of Gilead grows happily outside in sheltered positions. Plant in a well-drained soil in full sun, preferably against a warm, wind-protecting wall. The plant has an upright habit but spreads at the top, so planting distance from other plants should be approximately 1m (3ft).

It is a tender plant which may need protection in cooler climates. If you get frosts lower than –2°C (29°F) protect the plant for the winter, either by bringing it into a cool greenhouse or conservatory or by covering in an agricultural fleece.

Harvest
Pick leaves for drying before the flowers open, when they will be at their most aromatic.

Either pick flowers when just coming into bloom and dry, or wait until flowering is over and collect the black flower heads (good for winter arrangements).

Seeds are ready for extraction when you can hear the flower heads rattle. Store in an airtight container to sow in the spring.

CONTAINER GROWING

Balm of Gilead makes an excellent container plant. A 23–25cm (9–10in) pot will be required for a plant to reach maturity. Use a free-draining compost with bark and grit. Liquid feed a mature plant monthly throughout summer.

When grown in a conservatory, the scent of the leaves perfumes the air especially when the plant is watered or the sun shining on it. Flowers are long lasting and give a good show during the summer. Keep watering to the absolute minimum in the winter months.

MEDICINAL

Crush the leaves in your hand and inhale the aroma to clear your head.

Rub the leaves on skin to stop being bitten by mosquitoes.

Said to be an Aphrodisiac when applied....no comment.

OTHER USES
Dried leaves combine well in a spicy or woody potpourris with cedarwood chippings, rosewood, pineneedles, small fur cones, cypress oil and pine oil.

Add an infusion of the leaves to bath water for an invigorating bath.

Filipendula

MEADOWSWEET

Also known as Bridewort, Meadow Queen, Meadow-Wort, and Queen of the Meadow. From the family Rosaceae.

Meadowsweet can be found growing wild in profusion near streams and rivers, in damp meadows, fens and marshlands, or wet woodlands to 1,000m/3,300ft altitude.

It is a native of Europe and Asia that has been successfully introduced into, and is naturalized in, North America.

The generic name, *Filipendula,* comes from 'filum', meaning thread, 'pendulus', meaning hanging. This is said to describe the root tubers that hang, characteristically of the genus, on fibrous roots.

The common name, meadowsweet, is said to be derived from the Anglo-Saxon word 'medesweete', which itself owes its origin to the fact that the plant was used to flavour mead, a drink made from fermented honey.

It has been known by many other names. In Chaucer's *The Knight's Tale* it is Meadwort and was one of the ingredients in a drink called 'save'. It was also known as Bridewort, because it was strewn in churches for festivals and weddings and made into bridal garlands. In Europe it took its name Queen of the Meadow from the way the herb can dominate a low-lying, damp meadow. In America, it became Gravelroot or Joe Pie Weed (*Eupatorium purpureum*).

In the 16th century, when it was customary to strew floors with rushes and herbs (both to give warmth underfoot and to overcome smells and infections), it was a favourite of Queen Elizabeth I. She desired it above all other herbs in her chambers.

The sap contains a chemical of the same group as salicylic acid, an ingredient of aspirin. It was isolated for the first time in the 19th century by an Italian professor. When the drug company Bayer formulated acetylsalicylic acid, they called it aspirin after the old botanical name for meadowsweet, *Spirea ulmaria.*

SPECIES

Filipendula ulmaria
Meadowsweet
Hardy perennial. Ht 60-120cm (2-4ft), spread 60cm (2ft). Clusters of creamy-white flowers in mid-summer. Green leaf made up of up to 5 pairs of big leaflets separated by pairs of smaller leaflets.

Filipendula ulmaria Aurea
Golden Meadowsweet
Hardy perennial. Ht and spread 30cm (12in). Clusters of creamy-white flowers in mid-summer. Bright golden yellow, divided leaves in spring that turn a lime colour in summer. Susceptible to sun scorch.

Filipendula ulmaria 'Variegata'
Variegated Meadowsweet
Hardy perennial. Ht 45cm (18in) and spread 30cm (12in). Clusters of creamy-white flowers in mid-summer. Divided leaf, dramatically variegated green and yellow in spring. Fades a bit as the season progresses.

Filipendula vulgaris (hexapetala)
Dropwort
Hardy perennial. Ht 60-90cm (2-3ft), spread 45cm (18in). Summertime clusters of white flowers (larger than meadowsweet). Fern-like green leaves.

CULTIVATION

Propagation
Seed

ow in prepared seed or ug trays in the autumn. over lightly with compost ot Perlite) and winter utside under glass. Check om time to time that the ompost has not become dry this will inhibit rmination. Stratification is elpful but not essential. rmination should take ace in spring. When the edlings are large enough handle, plant out, 30cm 2in) apart, into a repared site.

Division
he golden and variegated rms are best propagated division. This is easily ne in the autumn. Dig up tablished plant and tease e plantlets apart; they parate easily. Either plant in a prepared site,)cm (12in) apart, or, if it is of the decorative varieties, ot up using the bark, peat ix of compost.

Pests and Diseases
eadowsweet rarely suffers om these.

Maintenance
Spring: Sow seeds if required.
Summer: Cut back after flowering.
Autumn: Divide established plants, sow seed for wintering outside.
Winter: No need for protection.

Garden Cultivation
Meadowsweet adapts well to the garden, but does prefer sun/semi-shade and a moisture retentive soil. If your soil is free-draining, mix in plenty of well-rotted manure and/or leaf mould, and plant in semi-shade.

Harvest
Gather young leaves for fresh or dry use before flowers appear. Pick flowers just as they open and use fresh or dry.

MEDICINAL

The whole plant is a traditional remedy for an acidic stomach.
  The fresh root is used in homeopathic preparations and is effective on its own in the treatment of diarrhoea.
  The flowers, when made into a tea, are a comfort to flu victims.

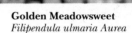

Golden Meadowsweet
Filipendula ulmaria Aurea

CONTAINER GROWING

Golden and variegated meadowsweet look very attractive in containers, but make sure the compost retains moisture. Position in partial shade to inhibit drying out and prevent sun scorch. The plant dies back in winter so leave it outside in a place where the natural weathers can reach it. If you live in an extremely cold area, protect the container from damage by placing in a site protected from continuous frost, but not warm. Liquid feed only twice during flowering, following manufacturer's instructions.

CULINARY

A charming, local vet who made all kinds of vinegars and pickles gave me to try meadowsweet vinegar. Much to my amazement it was lovely, and combined well with oil to make a different salad dressing, great when used with a flower salad.
  I am not a fan of meadow-sweet flower fritters so mention them only in passing. The flowers do however make a very good wine, and add flavour to meads and beers. The flowers can also be added to stewed fruit and jams, introducing a subtle almond flavour.
  Young leaves can be added to soups, but are not recommended for the faint-hearted!

OTHER USES

A black dye can be obtained from the roots by using a copper mordant.
  Use dried leaves and flowers in potpourris.

eadowsweet *Filipendula ulmaria*

Meadowsweet dye

'Purge me with Hyssop and I shall be clean'
(Psalm 51, verse 7).

Hyssopus

HYSSOP

From the family Labiatae.

Hyssop is a native of the Mediterranean region, where it grows wild on old walls and dry banks. It is found as a garden escapee elsewhere in Europe and has been cultivated in gardens for about the last 600 years. It was one of the herbs taken to the New World by the colonists to use in tea, in herbal tobacco and as an antiseptic.

There has been much to-ing and fro-ing about whether common hyssop is the one mentioned in the Bible. Some say it was oregano or savory. However, present thinking is that hyssop is flavour of the month especially since it has been discovered that the mould that produces penicillin grows on its leaf. This may have acted as an antibiotic protection when lepers were bathed in hyssop.

The Persians used distilled hyssop water as a body lotion to give a fine colour to their skin.

Hippocrates recommended hyssop for chest complaints, and today herbalists still prescribe it.

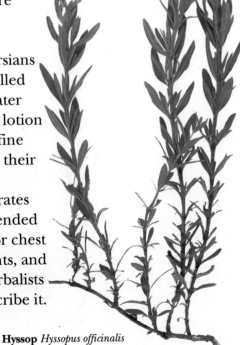

Hyssop *Hyssopus officinalis*

SPECIES

These are the common hyssops, readily available from nurseries and garden centres.

Hyssopus officinalis
Hyssop
Also known as Blue Hyssop Hardy semi-evergreen perennial. Ht 80cm (32in), spread 90cm (36in). Blue flowers from summer to early autumn. Small, narrow, lance-shaped leaves, aromatic and darkish green.

Hyssop *Hyssopus officinalis*

Hyssopus officinalis albus
White Hyssop
Semi-evergreen hardy perennial. Ht 80cm (32in), spread 90cm (36in). White flowers from summer to early autumn. Small, narrow, lance-shaped leaves, aromatic, and darkish green in colour.

Hyssopus officinalis ssp. aristatus
Rock Hyssop
Hardy, semi-evergreen, perennial. Ht 30cm (12in), spread 60cm (24in). Dark blue flowers from summer to early autumn. Small, narrow, lance-shaped leaves, aromatic and darkish green.

Hyssopus officinalis roseus
Pink Hyssop
Hardy, semi-evergreen, perennial. Ht 80cm (32in), spread 90cm (36in). Pink flowers from summer to early autumn. Small, narrow, lance-shaped leaves,

Pink Hyssop
Hyssopus officinalis roseus

CULTIVATION

Propagation
Seeds
In early spring sow the small seeds in plug or seed trays under protection, using the bark and peat mix of compost. Cover with Perlite. If very early in spring, a bottom heat of 15-21°C (60-70°F) would be beneficial. When the seedlings are large enough, either pot up or transplant into the garden after a period of hardening off. Plant at a distance of 30cm (12in) apart. All varieties can be grown from seed with the exception of rock hyssop, which can only be grown from cuttings. However, if you want a guaranteed pink or white hyssop, cuttings are a more reliable method.

Cuttings
In late spring, early summer take softwood cuttings from the new lush growth and non-flowering stems.

Pests and Diseases
This genial plant rarely suffers from pests or diseases.

Maintenance
Spring: Sow seeds. Trim mature plants. Trim hedges.
Summer: Dead-head flowers to maintain supply, trim after flowering to maintain shape. Trim hedges.
Autumn: Cut back only in mild areas.
Winter: Protect in cold, wet winters and temperatures that fall below -5°C (23°F). Use agricultural fleece, straw, bracken, etc.

Garden Cultivation
This attractive plant, which has only recently become popular again, likes to be planted in conditions similar to rosemary and thyme, a well-drained soil in a sunny position. The seeds can be sown directly into the ground in very late spring or early summer, when the soil is warm. Thin to 30cm (12in) apart if being grown as specimen plants. If for edging, 18cm (7in).
As all parts of the plant are pleasantly aromatic and the flowers very attractive, plant where it can be seen and brushed against. The flowers are also attractive to bees and butterflies. For these reasons hyssop makes a very good hedge or edging plant. Trim the top shoots to encourage bushy growth. In early spring, trim the plant into a tidy shape with scissors. To keep the plant flowering in summer, remove the dead heads. Cut back to 20cm (8in) in autumn in mild areas, or trim back after flowering in cold areas. Keep formal hedges well clipped during the growing season.

Harvest
Cut young leaves for drying in summer. The flowers should be picked during the summer too, when they are fully opened. The scent is generally improved with drying.

COMPANION PLANTING
Grow near cabbages to lure away cabbage whiteflies. Plant near vines to increase yield.

WARNING

Hyssop should not be used in cases of nervous irritability. Strong doses, particularly those of distilled essential oil, can cause muscular spasms. This oil should not be used in aromatherapy for highly-strung patients, as it can cause epileptic symptoms. Do not use continuously for extended periods. No form of hyssop should be taken during pregnancy.

Hyssop sugar syrup

CONTAINER GROWING

Hyssop is a lovely plant in containers. It is happy in plenty of sunshine and prefers a south-facing wall. It also likes dry conditions and its tough leaves are not affected by the fumes of city centres, making it ideal for window-boxes. Equally, it is good on a patio as the scent is lovely on a hot summer's evening. Give it a liquid feed only during the flowering period. Cut back after flowering to maintain shape.

CULINARY

The flowers are delicious tossed in a green salad. In small amounts, leaves aid digestion of fatty foods but as they are somewhat pungent use them sparingly. The herb has a slightly bitter, minty taste and is therefore good flavouring in salads or as an addition to game, meats and soups, stews and stuffings. A good idea is to add a teaspoon of chopped leaf to a Yorkshire pudding batter. Hyssop is still used in Gascony as one of the herbs in bouquet garni and for flavouring a concentrated purée of tomatoes preserved for the winter. It is used in continental sausages and also added to American fruit pies, ¼teaspoon hyssop being sprinkled over the fruit before the top crust goes on.
When making a sugar syrup for fruit, add a sprig of hyssop as you boil the sugar and water; it adds a pleasant flavour, and the sprig can be removed before adding the fruit. When making cranberry pie, use the leaves as a lining for the dish.

Basque-Style Chicken
Serves 6

1.5 kg (3lb 6oz) chicken
4 sweet peppers (2 red, 2 green)
Hyssop olive oil
5 tablespoons dry white wine
4 medium tomatoes, peeled and roughly chopped
6 onions
4 cloves of garlic
1 bouquet garni with a sprig of hyssop
salt and pepper

De-seed and slice the peppers into thin strips. Gently fry them in a small amount of oil until soft. Remove from pan and put to one side. Joint the chicken and gently fry in the oil, turning all the time. Transfer to a casserole, and season with salt and pepper, moisten with the wine, and leave over a gentle heat to finish cooking. Slice the onions and peel the garlic cloves, and soften without colouring in the olive oil in the frying pan. Then add the tomatoes, peppers and bouquet garni, and season. When reduced almost to a cream, turn into the casserole over the chicken and keep on a low heat until ready to serve, about a further 20-30 minutes.

Lavandula

LAVENDER

From the family Labiatae.

Native of the Mediterranean region, Canary Isles and India. Now cultivated in different regions of the world, growing in well-draining soil and warm, sunny climates.

Long before the world manufactured deodorants and bath salts, the Romans used lavender in their bath water; the word is derived from the Latin 'lava', to wash. It was the Romans who first introduced this plant to Britain and from then on monks cultivated it in their monastic gardens. Little more was recorded until Tudor times when people noted its fragrance and a peculiar power to ease stiff joints and relieve tiredness. It was brought in quantities from herb farms to the London Herb Market at Bucklesbury. 'Who will buy my lavender?' became perhaps the most famous of all London street cries.

It was used as a strewing herb for its insect-repellent properties and for masking household and street smells. It was also carried in nosegays to ward off the plague and pestilence. In France in the 17th century, huge fields of lavender were grown for the perfume trade. This has continued to the present day.

SPECIES

This is another big family of plants that are eminently worth collecting. I include here a few of my favourites, a few common, a few rare.

Lavandula Nana 'Alba'
Dwarf White Lavender
Hardy evergreen perennial. Ht and spread 30cm (12in). White flowers in summer. Green-grey narrow short leaves. This is the shortest growing lavender and is ideal for hedges.

Old English Lavender
Lavandula x intermedia 'Old English Group'

Lavandula angustifolia (spica, officinalis)
Common Lavender (English Lavender)
Hardy evergreen perennial. Ht 80 cm (32in), spread 1m (3ft). Mauve/purple flowers on a long spike in summer. Long, narrow, pale greenish-grey, aromatic leaves. One of the most popular and well known of the lavender family.

Lavandula angustifolia 'Alba'
White Lavender
Hardy evergreen perennial. Ht 70cm (28in), spread 80cm (32in). White flowers on a long spike in summer. Long, narrow, pale greenish-grey, aromatic leaves.

Lavandula angustifolia 'Bowles' variety
Lavender Bowles
Hardy evergreen perennial. Ht and spread 60cm (24in). Light blue flowers on a medium size spike in summer. Medium-length, narrow grey-greenish, aromatic leaves.

Lavandula angustifolia 'Folgate'
Lavender Folgate
Hardy evergreen perennial. Ht and spread 45cm (18in). Purple flowers on a medium spike in summer. Leaves as above.

Lavandula angustifolia 'Hidcote'
Lavender Hidcote
Hardy evergreen perennial. Ht and spread 45cm (18in). Dark blue flowers on a medium spike in summer. Fairly short, narrow, aromatic grey-greenish leaves. One of the most popular lavenders. Often used in hedging, planted at a distance of 30-40 cm (12-16 in).

Lavandula angustifolia 'Loddon Blue'
Lavender Loddon Blue
Hardy evergreen perennial. Ht and spread 45cm (18in). Pale blue flowers on a medium-length spike in summer. Fairly short, narrow grey-greenish, aromatic leaves. Good compact habit. There is another variety called 'Loddon Pink' – same size, same height, with pale pink flowers.

Lavender Hidcote *Lavandula*
angustifolia 'Hidcote'

Lavandula angustifolia 'Munstead'

Lavender Dwarf Munstead
Hardy evergreen
perennial. Ht and spread
5cm (18in). Purple/blue
flowers on a fairly short
spike in summer. Medium
length, greenish-grey,
narrow, aromatic leaves.
This is now a common
lavender and used often
in hedging, planted at a
distance of 30-40cm
(12-16in).

Lavandula angustifolia 'Rosea'

Lavender Pink/Rosea
Hardy evergreen
perennial. Ht and spread
5cm (18in). Pink flowers
in summer. Medium
length greenish-grey,
narrow, aromatic leaves.

Lavandula dentata

Fringe Lavender
sometimes called French
Lavender)
Half-hardy evergreen
perennial. Ht and spread
60cm (24in). Pale blue/
mauve flowers from
summer to early autumn.
Highly aromatic, serrated,
pale green, narrow leaves.
This plant is a native of
southern Spain and the
Mediterranean region and
needs protecting in cold
damp winters. It is ideal to
bring inside into a cool
room in early autumn as a
flowering pot plant.

Lavandula x intermedia Dutch group

Lavender Vera
Hardy evergreen perennial.
Ht and spread 45cm (18in).
Purple flowers in summer
on fairly long spikes. Long
greenish-grey, narrow,
aromatic leaves.

Lavandula x intermedia 'Grappenhall'

Lavender Grappenhall
Hardy evergreen perennial.
Ht and spread 1m (3ft).
Large pale mauve flowers on
long spikes in summer. The
flowers are much more open
than other species. Long
greenish-grey, narrow,
aromatic leaves.

Lavandula x intermedia 'Old English Group'

Old English Lavender
Hardy evergreen perennial.
Ht and spread 60cm (24in).
Light lavender blue flowers
on long spikes. Long,
narrow, silver/grey/green,
aromatic leaves.

French Lavender
Lavandula Stoechas

Lavandula x intermedia 'Seal'

Lavender Seal
Hardy evergreen perennial.
Ht 90cm (3ft), spread 60cm
(24in). Long flower stems,
mid-purple. Long, narrow,
silver/grey/green aromatic
leaves.

Lavandula x intermedia 'Twickel Purple'

Lavender Twickel Purple
Hardy evergreen perennial.
Ht and spread 50cm (20in).
Pale purple flowers on fairly
short spike. Medium length,
greenish-grey, narrow,
aromatic leaves. Compact
grower.

Lavender Pedunculata
Lavandula stoechas spp pedunculata

Lavandula lanata

Woolly Lavender
Hardy evergreen perennial.
Ht 50 cm (20in), spread
45cm (18in). Deep purple
flowers on short spikes.
Short, soft, narrow, silver-
grey aromatic foliage.

Lavandula pinnata

Lavender Pinnata
Half-hardy evergreen
perennial. Ht and spread
50cm (20in). The flower
spikes are a mixture of **L.
angustifolia** and **L. stoechas**,
purple in colour. Leaves are
fern-like, grey, and slightly
aromatic. Could be easily
mistaken for an **artemisia**.
Protect in winter.

Lavandula Stoechas

French Lavender
(sometimes called Spanish
Lavender)
Hardy evergreen perennial.
Ht 50cm (20in). Spread
60cm (24in). Attractive
purple bracts in summer.
Short, narrow, grey/green,
aromatic leaves.

Lavandula stoechas alba

White French Lavender
As **L. Stoechas** except white
bracts in summer.

Lavendula stoechas spp pedunculata

Lavender Pedunculata
(sometimes known as
Papillon)
Half-hardy evergreen
perennial. Ht and spread
60cm (24in). These
attractive purple bracts have
an extra centre tuft, which is
mauve and looks like two
rabbit ears. The aromatic
leaves are very narrow, grey
and longer than the
ordinary **stoechas**. Protect in
winter.

Lavandula viridis

Lavender Viridis
Half-hardy evergreen
perennial. Ht and spread
60cm (24in). This unusual
plant has green bracts with a
cream centre tuft. The
leaves are green, narrow,
and highly aromatic. Protect
in winter.

Lavenders – Small (grow to 45-50cm/18-20in)

*Lavender Folgate, Lavender
Hidcote, Lavender Lodden
Pink, Lavender Lodden Blue,
Lavender Munstead, Lavender
Dwarf White, Lavender Twickle
Purple.*

Lavenders – Medium (grow to 60cm/24in)

*Lavender Bowles, Lavender Old
English.*

Lavenders – Big (70cm/28in and above)

*Lavender Grappenhall,
Lavender White, Lavender Seal.*

Half-hardy Lavenders

*Lavender Dentata (50cm/
20in), Lavender Lanata
(50cm/20in), Lavender
Pinnata (50cm/20in),
Lavender Stoechas (50cm/
20in), Lavender Stoechas Alba
(50cm/20in), Lavender
Stoechas Pendunculata (60cm/
24in), Lavender Viridis (50cm/
20in).*

Fringe Lavender
Lavandula dentata

CULTIVATION

Propagation
Seed
Lavender can be grown from seed but it tends not to be true to species, with the exception of **Lavender Stoechas**.

Seed should be sown fresh in the autumn on the surface of a seed or plug tray and covered with Perlite. It germinates fairly readily with a bottom heat of 4-10°C (40-50°F). Winter the seedlings in a cold greenhouse or cold conservatory with plenty of ventilation. In the spring, prick out and pot on using the bark, peat, grit mix of compost. Let the young plant establish a good size root ball before planting out in a prepared site in the early summer. For other species you will find cuttings much more reliable.

Cuttings
Take softwood cuttings from non-flowering stems in spring. Root in bark, peat, grit mix of compost. Take semi-hardwood cuttings in summer or early autumn from the strong new growth. Once the cuttings have rooted well, it is better to pot them up and winter the young lavenders in a cold greenhouse or conservatory

Lavender viridis
Lavandula viridis

rather than plant them out in the first winter. In the spring, plant them out in well-drained, fertile soil, at a distance of 45-60cm (18-24in) apart or 30cm (12in) apart for an average hedge.

Layering
This is easily done in the autumn. Most hardy lavenders respond well to this form of propagation.

Pests and Diseases
One of the chief pests of lavenders are the cuckoo spit insects and the caterpillars of several types of moth. Cure cuckoo spit by spraying away the foamy white spit with water. Then use a horticultural liquid soap to remove the bugs and caterpillars (follow manufacturer's instructions).

The flowers in wet seasons may be attacked by grey mould and/or botrytis. This can occur all too readily after a wet winter. Cut back the infected parts as far as possible, again remembering not to cut into the old wood if you want it to shoot again.

There is another fungus (**Phoma lavandulae**) which attacks the stems and branches causing wilting and death of the affected branches. If this occurs dig up the plant immediately and destroy, keeping it well away from any other lavender bushes.

Maintenance
Spring: Give a spring hair cut.
Summer: Trim after flowering. Take cuttings.
Autumn: Sow seed. Cut back in early autumn, never into the old wood. Protect all the half-hardy lavenders. Bring containers inside.
Winter: Check seedlings for disease. Keep watering to a minimum.

Garden Cultivation
Lavender is one of the most popular plants in today's herb garden and is particularly useful in borders, edges, as internal hedges, and on top of dry walls. All the species need an open sunny position and a well-drained, fertile soil. But it will adapt to semi-shade as long as the soil conditions are met, otherwise it will die in winter. If you have very cold winter temperatures, it is worth container growing.

The way to maintain a lavender bush is to trim to shape every year in the spring, remembering not to cut into the old wood as this will not re-shoot. After flowering, trim back to the leaves. In the early autumn trim again, making sure this is well before the first autumn frosts. Otherwise the new growth will be too soft and be damaged. By trimming this way, you will keep the bush neat and encourage it to make new growth, so stopping it becoming woody.

If you have inherited a straggly mature plant then give it a good cut back in autumn, followed by a second cut in the spring and then adopt the above routine. If the plant is aged, I would advise that you propagate some of the autumn cuts, so preserving the plant if all else fails.

Harvest
Gather the flowers just as they open, and dry on open trays or by hanging in small bunches.

Pick the leaves any time for use fresh, or before flowering if drying.

Lavender sachets can be used to make good presents or used as moth repellent

CONTAINER GROWING

you have low winter
temperatures, lavenders
cannot be treated as a hardy
evergreen. Treated as a
container plant, however, it
can be protected in winter
and enjoyed just as well in
the summer. Choose
containers to set the
lavender off; they all suit
terracotta. Use a well-
drained compost – the peat,
bark, grit mix suits them
well. The ideal position is
sun, but all lavenders will
cope with partial shade,
though the aroma can be
impaired.
Feed regularly through the
flowering season with liquid
fertilizer, following the
manufacturer's instructions.
Allow the compost to dry out
in winter (not totally, but
nearly), and slowly reintro-
duce watering in spring.

CULINARY

Lavender has not been used
much in cooking, but as
there are many more
adventurous cooks around, I
am sure it will be used
increasingly in the future.
Use the flowers to flavour a
herb jelly, or a vinegar.
Equally the flowers can be
crystallized.

Lavender Biscuits

100g/4oz butter
50g/2oz caster sugar
175g/6oz self-raising flour
2 tablespoons fresh chopped
lavender leaves
1 teaspoon lavender flowers
removed from spike

Lavender biscuits

Cream the sugar and butter
together until light. Add the
flour and lavender leaves to
the butter mixture. Knead
well until it forms a dough.
Gently roll out on a lightly
floured board. Scatter the
flowers over the rolled
dough and lightly press in
with the rolling pin. Cut into
small rounds with cutter.
Place biscuits on a greased
baking sheet. Bake in a hot
oven 450°F 230°C, Gas mark
7 for 10-12 minutes until
golden and firm. Remove at
once and cool on a wire tray.

Lavender herb jelly

MEDICINAL

*Throughout history,
lavender has been used
medicinally to soothe,
sedate and suppress.
Nowadays it is the
essential oil that is in
great demand.*

*The oil was traditionally
inhaled to prevent vertigo
and fainting. It is an
excellent remedy for burns
and stings, and its strong
antibacterial action helps
to heal cuts. The oil also
kills diphtheria and
typhoid bacilli as well as
streptococcus and
pneumococcus.*

*Add 6 drops of oil to
bath water to calm
irritable children and
help them sleep. Place
1 drop on the temple for a
headache relief. Blend for
use as a massage oil in
aromatherapy for throat
infections, skin sores,
inflammation, rheumatic
aches, anxiety, insomnia
and depression. The best
oil is made
from
distillation,
and may be
bought
from many
shops.*

OTHER USES

Rub fresh flowers onto skin
or pin a sprig on clothes to
discourage flies. Use flowers
in potpourri, herb pillows,
and linen sachets, where it
makes a good moth
repellent.

Mentha
MINT
From the family Labiatae.

The *Mentha* family is a native of Europe that has naturalized in many parts of the world, including North America, Australia and Japan. Mint has been cultivated for its medicinal properties since ancient times and has been found in Egyptian tombs dating back to 1,000 BC. The Japanese have been growing it to obtain menthol for at least 2,000 years. In the Bible the Pharisees collected tithes in mint, dill and cumin. Charlemagne, who was very keen on herbs, ordered people to grow it. The Romans brought it with them as they marched through Europe and into Britain, from where it found its way to America with the settlers.

Its name was first used in Greek mythology. There are two different stories, the first that the nymph Minthe was being chatted up by Hades, god of the Underworld. His queen Sephony became jealous and turned her into the plant, mint. The second that Minthe was a nymph beloved by Pluto, who transformed her into the scented herb after his jealous wife took umbrage.

SPECIES

The mint family is large and well known. I have chosen a few to illustrate the diversity of the species.

Mentha arvensis var. piperascens
Japanese Peppermint
Hardy perennial. Ht 60cm-1m (2-3ft), spread 60cm (24in) and more. Loose purplish whorls of flowers in summer. Leaves, downy, oblong, sharply toothed and green grey; they provides an oil (90 per cent menthol), said to be inferior to the oil produced by **M. piperita**. This species is known as English mint in Japan.

Mentha aquatica
Water Mint
Hardy perennial. Ht 15-60cm (6-24in), spread indefinite. Pretty purple/lilac flowers, all summer. Leaves soft, slightly downy, mid-green in colour. The scent can vary from a musty mint to a strong peppermint. This should be planted in water or very wet marshy soil. It can be found growing wild around pounds and streams.

Mentha x gracilis (Mentha x gentilis)
Ginger Mint
Also known as Scotch Mint. Hardy perennial. Ht 45cm (18in), spread 60cm (24in). The stem has whorls of small, 2-lipped, mauve flowers in summer. The leaf is variegated, gold/green with serrated edges. The flavour is a delicate, warm mint that combines well in salads and tomato dishes.

Mentha longifolia
Buddleia Mint
Hardy perennial. Ht 80cm (32in), spread indefinite. Long purple/mauve flowers that look very like buddleia (hence its name). Long grey-green leaves with a musty minty scent. Very good plant for garden borders.

Mentha x piperita
Peppermint
Also known as Mentha d'Angleterre, Mentha Anglais, Pfefferminze and Englisheminze. Hardy perennial. Ht 30-60cm (12-24in), spread indefinite. Pale purple flowers in summer. Pointed leaves, darkish green with a reddish tinge, serrated edges. Very peppermint scented. This is the main medicinal herb of the genus. There are 2 species worth looking out for – black peppermint, with leaves much darker, nearly brown, and white peppermint, with leaves green, tinged with reddish brown.

above: **Ginger mint**
Mentha x gracilis

Mentha x piperita citrata
Eau de Cologne Mint
Also known as Orange Mint and Bergamot Mint. Hardy perennial. Ht 60-80cm (24-32in), spread indefinite. Purple/mauve flowers in summer. Purple tinged, roundish, dark green leaves. A delicious scent that has been described as lemon, orange, bergamot, lavender, as well as eau de cologne. This plant is a vigorous grower. Use in fruit dishes with discretion. Best use is in the bath.

Mentha x piperita citrata 'Basil'
Basil Mint

Hardy perennial. Ht 45-60cm (18-24in), spread indefinite. Purple/mauve flowers in summer. Leaves green with a reddish tinge, more pointed than Eau de cologne. The scent is unique, a sweet and spicy mint scent that combines well with tomato dishes, especially pasta.

Mentha x piperita citrata 'Lemon'
Lemon Mint

Hardy perennial. Ht 45-60cm (18-24in), spread indefinite. Purple whorl of flowers in summer. Green serrated leaf, refreshing minty lemon scent. Good as a mint sauce, or with fruit dishes.

Mentha pulegium
Pennyroyal

Hardy semi-evergreen perennial Ht 15cm (6in) creeper, spread indefinite. Mauve flowers in spring. Bright green leaves, very strong peppermint scent. There is so much to write bout this plant, it has got its wn section, see pages 20-21.

Mentha requienii
Corsican Mint

Also known as Rock mint. Hardy semi-evergreen perennial. Ground cover, spread indefinite. Tiny purple flowers throughout the summer. Tiny bright green leaves, which, when crushed, smell strongly of peppermint. Suits a rock rden or paved path, grows aturally in cracks of rocks. eeds shade and moist soil.

Mentha spicata
Spearmint

Also known as Garden mint and Common mint. Hardy perennial. Ht 45-60cm (18-24in), spread indefinite. Purple/mauve flowers in summer. Green pointed leaves with serrated edges. The most widely grown of all mints. Good for mint sauce, mint jelly, mint julep.

Mentha spicata crispa
Curly Mint

Hardy perennial. Ht 45-60cm (18-24in), spread indefinite. Light mauve flowers in spring. When I first saw this mint I thought it had a bad attack of aphid, but it has grown on me! The leaf is bright green and crinkled, its serrated edge slightly frilly. Flavour very similar to spearmint, so good in most culinary dishes.

Mentha sauveolens 'Variegata'
Pineapple Mint

Mentha spicata 'Moroccan'
Moroccan Mint

Hardy perennial. Ht 45-60cm (18-24in), spread indefinite. White flowers in summer. Bright green leaves with a texture and excellent mint scent. This is the one I use for all the basic mint uses in the kitchen. A clean mint flavour and scent, lovely with yoghurt and cucumber.

Mentha sauveolens
Apple Mint

Hardy perennial. Ht 60cm-1m (2-3ft), spread indefinite. Mauve flowers in summer. Roundish hairy leaves. Tall vigorous grower. Gets its name from its scent, which is a combination of mint and apples. More subtle than some mints, so good in cooking.

Mentha sauveolens 'Variegata'
Pineapple Mint

Hardy perennial. Ht 45-60cm (18-24in), spread indefinite. Seldom produces flowers, all the energy going into producing very pretty cream and green, slightly hairy leaves that look good in the garden. Not a rampant mint. Grows well in hanging baskets.

Apple mint *Mentha suaveolens*

Buddleia mint
Mentha longifolia

Mentha x villosa alopcuroides 'Bowles Mint'
Bowles Mint

Hardy perennial. Ht 60cm-1m (2-3ft), spread indefinite. Mauve flowers, round, slightly hairy green leaves, vigorous grower. Sometimes called incorrectly Applemint. Has acquired reputation as 'The Connoisseur's Culinary Mint'. Not sure I agree, but mint tastes do vary.

above: **Corsican mint**
Mentha requienii

Pycnathemum pilosum
Mountain Mint

Hardy perennial. Ht 90cm (3ft), spread 60cm (2ft). Knot-like white/pink flowers, small and pretty in summer. Leaves long, thin, pointed, and grey-green with a good mint scent and flavour. Not a **Mentha**, so therefore not a true mint, and does not spread. Looks very attractive in a border, and is to butterflies. Any soil will support it provided not too rich.

Ginger mint
Mentha x gracilis

CULTIVATION

Propagation
Seed
The seed on the market is not worthwhile – leaf flavour is inferior and quite often it does not run true to species.

Cuttings
Root cuttings of mint are very easy. Simply dig up a piece of root. Cut it where you can see a little growing node (each piece will produce a plant) and place the cuttings either into a plug or seed tray. Push them into the compost (bark, peat mix). Water in and leave. This can be done any time during the growing season. If taken in spring, in about 2 weeks you should see new shoots emerging through the compost.

Division
Dig up plants every few years and divide, or they will produce root runners all over the place. Each bit of root will grow, so take care. Corsican mint does not set root runners. Dig up a section in spring and divide by easing the plant apart and replanting.

Pests and Diseases
Mint rust appears as little rusty spots on the leaves. Remove them immediately, otherwise the rust will wash off into the soil and the spores spread to other plants. One sure way to be rid is to burn the affected patch. This effectively sterilizes the ground.

Another method, which I found in an old gardening book, is to dig up the roots in winter when the plants are dormant, and clean off the soil under a tap. Heat some water to a temperature of 40-46°C (105°-115°F) and pour into a bowl. Place the roots in the water for 10 minutes. Remove the runners and wash at once in cold water. Replant in the garden well away from the original site.

Maintenance
Spring: Dig up root if cuttings are required. Split established plants if need be.
Summer: Give plants a hair cut to promote new growth. Control the spread of unruly plants.
Autumn: Dig up roots for forcing. Bring in containers.
Winter: Sterilize roots if rust evident during growing season.

Garden Cultivation
Mint is one of those plants that will walk all over the plot if not severely controlled. Also, mint readily hybridizes itself, varying according to environmental factors.

If choosing a plant in a nursery or garden centre rub the leaf first to check the scent. Select a planting site in sun or shade but away from other mints. Planted side by side they seem to loose their individual scent and flavour.

To inhibit spread, sink a large bottomless container (bucket or bespoke frame) in a well-drained and fairly rich soil to a depth of at least 30cm (12in), leaving a small ridge above soil level. Plant the mint in the centre.

Harvest
Pick the leaves for fresh use throughout the growing season. Pick leaves for drying or freezing before the mint flowers.

COMPANION PLANTING

Spearmint or peppermint planted near roses will deter aphids. Buddleia mint will attract hover flies.

OTHER USES

Pick a bunch of eau de cologne mint, tie it up with string, and hang it under the hot water tap when you are drawing a bath. You will scent not only your bath, but the whole house. It is very uplifting (unless you too have a young son, who for some reason thinks it is 'gross').

Curly mint
Mentha spicata 'Crispa' See p

Chocolate mint mousse

CONTAINER GROWING (AND FORCING)

Mint is good in containers. Make sure the container is large enough, use a soil-based compost, and do not let the compost dry out. Feed regularly throughout the growing season with a liquid fertilizer. Place the container in semi-shade.

One good reason for growing mint in containers is to prolong the season. This is called forcing. In early autumn dig up some root. Fill a container, or wooden box lined with plastic, with compost. Lay the root down its length and cover lightly with compost. Water in and place in a light, warm glasshouse or warm conservatory (even the kitchen windowsill will do). Keep an eye on it, and fresh shoots should sprout within a couple of weeks. This is great for fresh mint sauce for Christmas.

MEDICINAL

Peppermint is aromatic, calmative, antiseptic, antispasmodic, anti-inflammatory, anti-bacterial, anti-parasitic, and is also a stimulant. It can be used in a number of ways for a variety of complaints including gastro-intestinal disorders where antispasmodic, anti-flatulent and appetite- promoting stimulation is required. It is particularly useful for nervous headaches, and as a way to increase concentration. Externally, peppermint oil can be used in a massage to relieve muscular pain.

WARNING

The oil may cause an allergic reaction. Avoid prolonged intake of inhalants from the oil, which must never be used by babies.

CULINARY

...th due respect to their ...isine, the French are ...ays rude about our 'mint ...uce with lamb'; they ...ckon it is barbaric. On the ...her side of the Channel ...ey use mint less than other ...untries in cooking. But ...wly, even in France, this ...rb is gaining favour. ...Mint is good in vinegars ...d jellies. Peppermint ...akes a great tea. And there ...e many many uses for mint ... cooking with fish, meat, ...ghurt, fruit, and so on. ...re is a recipe for ...ocoholics like me:

Chocolate Mint Mousse
Serves 2

100g (4oz) plain dark chocolate
2 eggs, separated
1 teaspoon instant coffee
1 teaspoon fresh chopped mint, either Moroccan, spearmint or curly
Whipped cream for decoration
4 whole mint leaves

Melt the chocolate either in a microwave, or in a double saucepan. When smooth and liquid, remove from heat. Beat egg yolks and add to the chocolate while hot (this will cook the yolks slightly). Add coffee and chopped mint.

Leave the mixture to cool for about 15 minutes. Beat the egg whites (not too stiff) and fold them into the cooling chocolate mixture. Spoon into containers. When you are ready to serve put a blob of whipped cream in the middle and garnish with whole leaves.

Black peppermint tea

Monarda

BERGAMOT

Also known as Oswego Tea, Bee Balm, Blue Balm, High Balm, Low Balm, Mountain Balm and Mountain Mint. From the family Labiatae.

This beautiful plant with its flamboyant flower is a native of North America and is now grown horticulturally in many countries throughout the world.

The species name Monarda honours the Spanish medicinal botanist Dr Nicholas Monardes of Seville who, in 1569, wrote a herbal on the flora of America. The common name, Bergamot, is said to have come from the scent of the crushed leaf which resembles the small bitter Italian Bergamot orange (*Citrus bergamia*), from which oil is produced that is used in aromatherapy, perfumes and cosmetics.

The wild or purple Bergamot (*Monarda fistulosa*) grows around the Oswego river district near Lake Ontario in the United States. The Indians in this region used it for colds and bronchial complaints as it contains the powerful antiseptic, Thymol. They also made tea from it, hence Oswego Tea that was drunk in many American households, replacing Indian tea, following the Boston Tea Party of 1773.

SPECIES

There are many species and cultivars of Bergamot, too many to mention here, so I have included some from each of the species.

Monarda 'Beauty of Cobham'
Bergamot Beauty of Cobham
Hardy perennial. Ht 75cm (30in), spread 45cm (18in). Attractive dense 2-lipped pale pink flowers throughout summer. Toothed mid-green aromatic leaves.

Monarda 'Blaustrumpf'
Bergamot Blue Stocking
Hardy perennial. Ht 80cm (32in), spread 45cm (18in). Attractive purple flowers throughout summer. Aromatic, green, pointed foliage.

Monarda 'Cambridge Scarlet'
Bergamot Cambridge Scarlet
Hardy perennial. Ht 1m (3ft), spread 45cm (18in). Striking rich red flowers throughout summer. Aromatic, slightly hairy leaves of a mid-green colour.

Monarda didyma
Bergamot (Bee Balm Red)
Hardy perennial. Ht 80cm (2.5ft), spread 45cm (18in). Fantastic red flowers throughout summer. Aromatic, mid-green foliage.

Monarda punctata 'Schneewittchen'
Bergamot Snow Maiden
Hardy perennial. Ht 80cm (2.5ft), spread 45cm (18in). Very attractive white flowers throughout summer. Aromatic, mid-green, pointed leaves.

Monarda citriodora 'Croftway Pink'
Bergamot Croftway Pink
Hardy perennial. Ht 1m (3ft), spread 45cm (18in). Soft pink flowers throughout summer. Aromatic green leaves.

Monarda menthifolia 'Prarienacht'
Bergamot Prarie Night
Hardy perennial. Ht 1m
(3ft), spread 45cm (18in).
Attractive purple flowers
throughout summer.
Aromatic, mid-green,
pointed leaves.

CULTIVATION

Propagation
Seed
nly species will grow true
om seed. Cultivars (i.e.
med varieties) will not.
ow the very small seed
doors in the spring on the
rface of either seed or
ug trays or on individual
ts. Cover with Perlite.
rmination is better with
ded warmth 21°C (65°F).
in or transplant the
ongest seedlings when
ge enough to handle.
rden off. Plant in the
rden at a distance of 45cm
8in) apart.

Cuttings
ke first shoots in early
mmer, as soon as they are
-10cm (3-4in) long.

Division
vide in early spring. Either
ow on in pots, or replant
the garden, making sure
e site is well prepared with
ll-rotted compost.
nting distance from other
nts 45cm (18in).

Pests and Diseases
rgamot is prone to
wdery grey mildew. At the
st sign remove leaves. If it
ts out of hand cut the
nt back to ground level.
oung plants are a *bonne
che* for slugs!

Maintenance
ing: Sow seeds of species.
vide roots. Dig up 3-year-
plants, divide and
lant.
mmer: Take cuttings of
tivars and species, if
sired.

Autumn: Cut back to the
ground, and give a good
feed with manure or
compost.
Winter: All perennial
Bergamots die right back in
winter. In hard winters
protect with a mulch.

Garden Cultivation
Bergamot is a highly
decorative plant with long-
lasting, distinctively fragrant
flowers that are very
attractive to bees, hence
the country name Bee Balm.
  All grow well in moist,
nutrient-rich soil, preferably
in a semi-shady spot;
deciduous woodland is ideal.
However, they will tolerate
full sun provided the soil
retains moisture. Like many
other perennials bergamot
should be dug up and
divided every three years,
and the dead centre
discarded.

Harvest
Pick leaves as desired for use
fresh in the kitchen. For
drying, harvest before the
flower opens.
  Cut flowers for drying as
soon as fully opened. They
will dry beautifully and keep
their colour.
  It is only worth collecting
seed if you have species
plants situated well apart in
the garden. If near one
another, cross-pollination
will make the seed variable –
very jolly provided you don't
mind unpredictably mixed
colours. Collect the flower
heads when they turn
brown.

CONTAINER GROWING

Bergamot is too tall for a
window box, but it can look
very attractive growing in a
large pot, say 35-45 cm (14-
18in) across, or tub as long
as the soil can be kept moist
and the plant be given some
afternoon shade.

CULINARY

Pick the small flower petals
separately and scatter over a
green salad at the last
moment. Put fresh leaf in
China tea for an Earl Grey
flavour, and into wine cups
and lemonade. The
chopped leaves can be
added sparingly to salads
and stuffings, and can also
be used in jams and jellies.

Pork Fillets with Bergamot Sauce
Serves 2

2 large pork fillets
75g (3oz/6 tablespoons) butter
2 shallots, very finely chopped
40g (1½oz/2½ tablespoons
  flour
4 tablespoons dry white wine
3½ tablespoons chopped
  bergamot leaves
salt, black pepper
1 tablespoon double cream

Pre-heat the oven to 200°C/
400°F/Gas mark 6.
  Wash the fillets of pork. Pat
dry, season and smear with
half the butter.
  Roast in a shallow greased
tin for 25 minutes. Allow to
rest for 5 minutes before
slicing. Arrange slices in
warmed serving dish.
  Prepare this sauce while
the fillets are in the oven:
Sweat the shallots in half the
butter until soft. Stir in the
flour and cook for about a
minute, stirring all the time.
Whisk in the stock. Simmer
until it thickens, stirring
occasionally. Then slowly
add the wine and 3
tablespoons of the chopped
bergamot. Simmer for
several minutes then season
to taste. Remove from heat,
stir in the cream, pour over
arranged pork slices garnish
with remaining chopped
bergamot.
  Serve with mashed potato,
and fresh green broccoli.

OTHER USES
Because the dried Bergamot
flowers keep their fragrance
and colour so well, they are
an important ingredient in
potpourris.
  The oil is sometimes used
in perfumes, but should not
be confused with the
similarly smelling bergamot
orange.

MEDICINAL

*Excellent herb tea to relieve
nausea, flatulence, menstrual
pain and vomiting.
  Aromatherapists have
found bergamot oil good for
depression, as well as
helping the body to fight
infections.*

Myrtus Communis

MYRTLE

From the family Myrtaceae.

Myrtle *Myrtus communis* **in flower**

SPECIES

Myrtus communis
Myrtle
Half-hardy evergreen perennial. Ht and spread 2-3m (6-10ft). Fragrant white flowers from spring to mid-summer, each with a dense cluster of golden stamens; followed by dark, purple-black fruits. The leaves are oval, glossy, dark green and aromatic.

Myrtle communis 'Variegata'
Variegated Myrtle
Half-hardy evergreen perennial. Ht and spread 1-2m (3-6ft). Fragrant white flowers from spring to mid-summer, each with a hint of pink, and a dense cluster of golden stamens; followed by dark, purple-black fruits. Leaves are oval and dark green with silver variegation, and a pink tinge in autumn.

Myrtle communis ssp. tarentina
Tarentina Myrtle
Half-hardy evergreen perennial. Ht and spread 1-2m (3-6ft). Fragrant white flowers from spring to mid-summer, each with a dense cluster of golden stamens; followed by dark, purple-black fruits. Leaves are small and oval, dark green and aromatic. This myrtle is a good hedge in mild areas. Plant 60cm (24in) apart.

Myrtus communis tarenti 'Variegata'
Variegated Tarentina Myrt
Half-hardy evergreen perennial. Ht 1m (3ft), spread 60cm (2ft). Fragra white flowers from spring mid-summer, each with hint of pink and a dens cluster of golden stamen followed by dark, purple black fruits. Leaves are small, oval, and dark gree with silver variegation, an pink tinge in autumn.

I have included the following two because the have only recently been r classified as **Luma** and ar worth looking out for.

Luma chequen (Myrtus chequen)
Half-hardy evergreen perennial. Ht and sprea 10m (30ft). Fragrant whi flowers from spring to mi summer, each with a den cluster of golden stamen followed by dark purple black fruits. The leaves ar more oblong with a point the end: glossy dark gree and aromatic.

Luma apiculata Glanleam Gold (Myrtus 'Glanleam Gold')
Half-hardy evergreen perennial. Ht and sprea 10m (30ft). Fragrant whi flowers from mid summer mid-autumn, each with a hint of pink and a dense cluster of golden stamen followed by red fruits whi darken to deep purple as they ripen. Leaves oval, bright green, edged with creamy yellow.

Myrtle comes from a fragrant genus that is widely distributed in warm temperate and tropical regions of the world.

Myrtle is a direct descendant of the Greek Myrtos, the herb of love. It has been dedicated to Venus and was planted all round her temples. The story goes that Venus transformed one of her priestess called Myrrh into myrtle in order to protect her from an over-eager suitor. Also, Venus herself wore a wreath of myrtle when she was given the Golden Apple by Paris in recognition of her beauty. When she arose out of the sea she was carrying a sprig of myrtle, and to this day it grows very well by the sea, flourishing in the salt air.

Subsequently it was considered an aphrodisiac, and brides carried it in their bouquets or wore wreaths of it at weddings to symbolize love and consistency.

Myrtle *Myrtus communis* **in berry**

Myrtle growing in a hedge

CULTIVATION

Propagation
Cuttings
...ke softwood cuttings in ...ring, semi-hardwood ...ttings in summer. As these ...e tender plants it is as well ... grow them on in pots for ...e first 2 years at least. If ...u live in an area where the ...nter temperatures fall ...ntinuously below 0°C ...2°F) – for variegated ...rieties 5°C (41°F) – it ...uld be better to leave ...em in their pots for the ...nter. Use the bark, peat, ...it mix of compost.

Pests and Diseases
... the majority of cases ...yrtles are free from pests ...d diseases, but susceptible ... root rot from over-
...tering.

Maintenance
...ring. Trim back growth to ...gain shape. Take softwood ...ttings.

Summer. Take semi-hardwood cuttings.
Autumn. Protect from early frosts.
Winter. Protect in the winter if you live in a frost area.

Garden Cultivation
This lovely, tender, aromatic shrub will grow in fertile well-drained soil in full sun. Where your winters are borderline, plant against a south or west facing wall to restrict the amount of water it receives from rain, and protect it from the winds. If a frost is forecast, cover lightly with an agricultural fleece.
   Trim back growth (where possible) to maintain shape in mid-spring after the frosts have finished.

Harvest
Pick leaves for sweetness and scent when myrtle is in flower; they can be used dried or fresh.
   Preserve the leaves in oil or vinegar for use in cooking.
   Pick flowers for drying just as they open.

CULINARY

Leaves can be added to pork for the final 10 minutes of roasting, or to lamb when barbecuing. They have a spicy flavour.
   After drying, the berries can be ground and used like juniper as a spice for game and venison.

MEDICINAL

The leaves have astringent and antiseptic properties. Rarely used medicinally, but a leaf decoction may be applied externally to bruises and haemorrhoids. Recent research has revealed a substance in myrtle that has an antibiotic action.

CONTAINER GROWING

This plant, when young, is well suited to containers. Use the bark, peat, grit mix of compost. As an evergreen plant, it looks attractive all year round. Place in a cold conservatory away from central heating. Water in the summer months, and allow the compost nearly to dry out in winter. Watch the watering at all times; if ever in doubt give it less rather than more. Feed with a liquid fertilizer during the flowering period.

OTHER USES

Every part of the shrub is highly aromatic and can be used dried in potpourris.

Myrtle potpourri

Nepeta

CATMINT

***Also known as Catnep, Catnip, Catrup, Catswart and Field Balm.
From the family Labiatae.***

Catmint *Nepeta racemosa*

Native to Europe and East and West Asia, but now naturalized in other temperate zones.

The species name may have derived from the Roman town Nepeti, where it was said to grow in profusion.

The Elizabethan herbalist, Gerard, recorded the source of its common name: 'They do call it *herba cataria* and *herba catti* because cats are very much delighted herewith for the smell of it is so pleasant unto them, that they rub themselves upon it and wallow or tumble in it and also feed on the branches and leaves very greedily.'

This herb has long been cultivated both for its medicinal and seasoning properties, and in the hippie era of the late '60s and '70s for its mildly hallucinogenic quality when smoked.

SPECIES

Nepeta cataria, **Nepeta x faassenii** and **Nepeta racemosa** are all called catmint, which can be confusing. However the first is the true herb with the medicinal and culinary properties and, just to be more confusing, is known also as dog mint!

Nepeta racemosa (mussinii)
Hardy perennial. Ht and spread 50cm (20in). Spikes of lavender blue/purple flowers from late spring to autumn. Small, mildly fragrant, greyish leaves. Marvellous edging plant for tumbling out over raised beds or softening hard edges of stone flags. Combines especially well with old-fashioned roses.

Nepeta camphorata
Hardy perennial. Ht and spread 60-75cm (24-30in). Very different from ordinary catmint and very fragrant. Tiny white blooms all summer. Small, silvery grey, aromatic foliage. Prefers a poor, well-drained, dryish soil, not too rich in nutrients, and full sun. However, it will adapt to most soils except wet and heavy.

Nepeta x faassenii
Hardy perennial. Ht and spread 45cm (18in). Loose spikes of lavender blue flowers from early summer to early autumn. Small greyish-green aromatic leaves form a bushy clump.

Nepeta cataria
Dog mint, Nep-in-a-hedge.
Hardy perennial. Ht 1m (3ft), spread 60cm (2ft). White to pale pink flower from early summer to ear autumn. Pungent aromati leaves. This plant is the tr herb. In the 17th century was used in the treatment barren women.

CULTIVATION

Propagation
Seed
Sow its small seed in spring or late summer, either where the plant is going to flower or onto the surface pots, plug or seed trays. Cover with Perlite. Gentle bottom heat can be of assistance. Germination takes from 10-20 days, depending on the time of year (faster in late summer Seed is viable for 5 years. When large enough to handle, thin the seedlings 30cm (12in). The seed of **camphorata** should be sow in autumn to late winter. This seed will usually flowe the following season.

Cuttings
Take softwood cuttings fro new growth in late spring through to mid-summer. D not choose flowering stems

Catmint 'Six Hills Giant'
Nepeta 'Six Hills Giant'

Catmint *Nepeta cataria*

Division

good method of
propagation particularly if a
plant is becoming invasive.
But beware of cats! The
smell of a bruised root is
irresistible. Cats have been
known to destroy a specimen
replanted after division. If
there are cats around,
protect the newly divided
plant.

Pests and Diseases

These plants are aromatic
and not prone to pests.
However, in cold wet
winters, they tend to rot off.

Maintenance

Spring: Sow seeds.
Summer: Sow seeds until late
in the season. Cut back hard
after flowering to encourage
a second flush.
Autumn: Cut back after
flowering to maintain shape
and produce new growth. If
your winters tend to be wet
and cold, pot up and winter
this herb in a cold frame.
Winter: Sow seeds of **Nepeta
camphorata**.

Garden Cultivation

The main problem with
catmint is the love cats have
for it. If you have ever seen a
cat spaced-out after feeding
(hence catnip) and rolling
on it, then you will
understand why cat lovers
love catmint, and why cat
haters who grow it get cross
with cat neighbours. The
reason why cats are enticed
is the smell; it reminds them
of the hormonal scent of
cats of the opposite sex.
With all this in mind, choose
your planting site carefully.
  Nepeta make very attractive
border or edging subjects.
They like a well drained soil,
sun, or light shade. The one
thing they dislike is a wet
winter, they may well rot off.
  Planting distance depends
on species, but on average
plant 50cm (20in) apart.
When the main flowering is
over, catmint should be cut
back hard to encourage a
second crop and to keep a
neat and compact shape.

Harvest

Whether you pick to use
fresh or to dry, gather leaves
and flowering tops when
young.

MEDICINAL

Nepeta cataria is now very
rarely used for medicinal
purposes. In Europe it is
sometimes used in a hot
infusion to promote
sweating. It is said to be
excellent for colds and flu
and children's infectious
diseases, such as measles. It
soothes the nervous system
and helps get a restless child
off to sleep. It also helps to
calm upset stomachs and
counters colic, flatulence
and diarrhoea.
  In addition, an infusion
can be applied externally to
soothe scalp irritations, and
the leaves and flowering tops
can be mashed for a poultice
to be applied to external
bruises.

COMPANION PLANTING

Planting **Nepeta cataria** near
vegetables deters flea beetle.

CONTAINER GROWING

N. x faassenii and **N.
racemosa** look stunning in
large terracotta pots. The
grey green of the leaves and
the blue-purple of the
flowers complement the
terracotta, and their
sprawling habit in flower
completes the picture. Use a
well-draining compost, such
as a peat, grit, bark mix.
Note: both varieties tend to
grow soft and leggy indoors.

OTHER USES

Dried leaves stuffed into toy
mice will keep kittens and
cats amused for hours.
  The scent of catnip is said
to repel rats, so put bunches
in hen and duck houses to
discourage them.
  The flowers of **Nepeta x
faassenii**, and **Nepeta
racemosa** are suitable for
formal displays.

Oenothera

EVENING PRIMROSE

Also known as Common Evening Primrose, Evening Star, Fever Plant, Field Primrose, King's Cure-all, Night Willowherb, Scabish, Scurvish, Tree Primrose, Primrose, Moths Moonflower and Primrose Tree. From the family Onagraceae.

A native of North America it was introduced to Europe in 1614 when botanists brought the plant from Virginia as a botanical curiosity. In North America it is regarded as a weed, elsewhere as a pretty garden plant.

The generic name, *Oenothera*, comes from the Greek 'oinos' (wine) and 'thera' (hunt). According to ancient herbals the plant was said to dispel the ill effects of wine, but both plant and seed have been used for other reasons – culinary and medicinal – by American Indians for hundreds of years. The Flambeau Ojibwe tribe were the first to realise its medicinal properties. They used to soak the whole plant in warm water to make a poultice to heal bruises and overcome skin problems. Traditionally, too, it was used to treat asthma, and its medicinal potential is still evolving. Oil of Evening Primrose is currently attracting considerable attention worldwide as a treatment for nervous disorders, in particular Multiple Sclerosis. There may well be a time in the very near future when the pharmaceutical industry will require fields of this beautiful plant to be grown on a commercial scale.

The common name comes from the transformation of its bedraggled daytime appearance into a fragrant, phosphorescent, pale yellow beauty with the opening of its flowers in the early evening. All this show is for one night only, however. Towards the end of summer the flowers tend to stay open all day long. (It is called Evening Star because the petals emit phosphorescent light at night.) Many strains of the plant came to Britain as stowaways in soil used as ballast in cargo ships.

Evening Primrose
Oenothera macrocarpa

SPECIES

Evening Primrose
Oenothera biennis

Oenothera biennis
Evening Primrose
Hardy biennial. Ht 90-120cm (3-4ft), spread 90cm (3ft). Large evening scented yellow flowers for most of the summer. Long green oval or lance-shaped leaves This is the medicinal herb, and the true herb.

Oenothera macrocarpa (missouriensis)
Hardy perennial. Ht 10cm (4in), spread 40cm (16in) or more. Large yellow bell-shaped flowers, sometimes spotted with red, open at sundown throughout the summer. The small to medium green leaves are of a narrow oblong shape.

Oenothera perennis (Pumi
Hardy perennial. Ht 15-60c (6-24in), spread 30cm (12i: Fragrant yellow funnel-shaped flowers all summe The green leaves are narr and spoon-shaped.

CULTIVATION

Propagation
Seeds

ow in early spring on the
urface of pots or plug trays,
r direct into a prepared site
 the garden. Seed is very
ne so be careful not to sow
 too thick. Use the
ardboard method. When
e weather has warmed
fficiently, plant out at a
istance of 30cm (12in)
art. Often the act of
ansplanting will encourage
e plant to flower the first
ar. It is a prolific self-
eder. So once introduced
 to the garden, it will stay.

Pests and Diseases
his plant rarely suffers
om pests or disease.

Maintenance
ring: Sow seed.
mmer: Dead head plants to
t down on self-seeding.
utumn: Dig up old roots of
cond-year growth of the
ennials.
inter: No need to protect.

Garden Cultivation
oose a well-drained soil in
dry, sunny corner for the
st results and sow the
eds in late spring to
oduce flowers the
llowing year. Thin the
edlings to 30cm (12in)
art, when large enough to
ndle. After the seed is set,
e plant dies. It is an
tremely tolerant plant,
ppy in most situations,
d I have known seedlings
pear in a stone wall, so be
ewarned.

Harvest
e leaves fresh as required.
st before flowering.
ck the flowers when in
d or when just open. Use
sh. Picked flowers will
vays close and are no good
 flower arrangements.

Collect the seeds as the
heads begin to open at the
end. Store in jar for sowing
in the spring.
Dig up roots and use fresh
as a vegetable or to dry.

CONTAINER GROWING

The lower growing varieties
are very good in window
boxes and tubs. Tall varieties
need support from other
plants or stakes. None is
suitable for growing indoors.

CULINARY

*It is a pot herb – roots,
stems, leaves, and even
flower buds may be eaten.
The roots can be boiled –
they taste like sweet
parsnips, or pickled and
tossed in a salad.*

MEDICINAL

Soon this plant will take its
place in the hall of herbal
fame.
It can have startling effects
on the treatment of pre-
menstrual tension. In 1981
at St Thomas's Hospital,
London, 65 women with
PMS were treated. 61 per
cent experienced complete
relief and 23 per cent partial
relief. One symptom, breast
engorgement, was especially
improved – 72 per cent of
women reported feeling
better. In November 1982,

Evening Primrose *Oenothera biennis*

an edition of the prestigious
medical journal *The Lancet*
published the results of a
double-blind crossover study
on 99 patients with ectopic
excema, which showed that
when high doses of Evening
Primrose Oil were taken,
about 43 per cent of the
patients experienced
improvement of their
eczema. Studies of the effect
of the oil on hyperactive
children also indicate that
this form of treatment is
beneficial.
True to the root of its
generic name, the oil does
appear to be effective in
counteracting alcohol
poisoning and preventing
hangovers. It can help
withdrawal from alcohol,
easing depression. It helps
dry eyes and brittle nails
and, when combined with
zinc, the oil may be used to
treat acne.
But it is the claim that it
benefits sufferers of multiple
sclerosis that has brought
controversy. It has been
recommended for MS
sufferers by Professor Field,
who directed MS research
for the UK Medical Research
Council.
Claims go further – that it
is effective in guarding
against arterial disease; the
effective ingredient, gami-
linolelic acid (GLA), is a
powerful anti-blood clotter,
that it aids weight-loss; a
New York hospital
discovered that people more

than 10 per cent above their
ideal body weight lost weight
when taking the oil. It is
thought that this occurs
because the GLA in Evening
Primrose Oil stimulates
brown fat tissue... and that
in perhaps the most
remarkable study of all,
completed in Glasgow Royal
Infirmary in 1987, it helped
60 per cent of patients
suffering from rheumatoid
arthritis. Those taking fish
oil, in addition to Evening
Primrose Oil, fared even
better.
The scientific explanation
for these extraordinary
results is that GLA is a
precursor of a hormone-like
substance called PGEI,
which has a wide range of
beneficial effects on the
body. Production of this
substance in some people
may be blocked. GLA has
also been found in oil
extracted from blackcurrant
seed and borage seed, both
of which are now a
commercial source of this
substance.

OTHER USES

Leaf and stem can be
infused to make an
astringent facial steam. Add
to hand cream as a softening
agent.

Pelargonium

SCENTED GERANIUMS

From the family Geraniaceae.

These form a group of marvellously aromatic herbs which should be used more. Originally native of South Africa, they are now widespread throughout many temperate countries, where they should be grown as tender perennials.

The generic name, *Pelargonium*, is said to be derived from 'pelargos', a stork. With a bit of imagination one can understand how this came about, the seed pods bear resemblance to a stork's bill.

Nearly all the species of scented geranium (the name is a botanical misnomer) came from the Cape of South Africa to England in the mid-17th century. The aromatic foliage found popular assent among Victorians, who used them as houseplants to scent the room. In the early 19th century the French perfumery industry recognized its commercial potential. Oil of Geranium is now not only an ingredient of certain perfumes for men, but also an essential oil in aromatherapy.

SPECIES

There are many different scented geraniums. I am mentioning a few typical of the species that I have a soft spot for. They are a very collectable plant.

Pelargonium 'Attar of Roses'
Half-hardy evergreen perennial. Ht 30-60cm (12-24in), spread 30cm (12in). Small pink flowers in summer. 3-lobed, mid-green leaves that smell of roses.

Pelargonium 'Atomic Snowflake'
Half-hardy evergreen perennial. Ht 30-60cm, (12-24in), spread 30cm (12in). Small pink flowers in summer. Intensely lemon-scented, roundish leaves with silver grey/green variegation.

Pelargonium capitatum
Half-hardy evergreen perennial. Ht 30-60cm (12-24in), spread 30cm (12in). Small mauve flowers in summer, irregular 3-lobed green leaves, rose scented. This is now mainly used to produce geranium oil for the perfume industry.

Pelargonium 'Chocolate Peppermint'
Half-hardy evergreen perennial. Ht 30-60cm (12-24in), spread 1m (3ft). Small white/pink flowers i summer. Large, rounded, shallowly lobed leaves, velvety green with brown marking and a strong scen of chocolate peppermints This is a fast grower so pinc out growing tips to keep shape.

Pelargonium 'Clorinda'
Half-hardy evergreen perennial. Ht and spread 1 (3ft). Large pink attractive flowers in summer. Large rounded leaves, mid-green and eucalyptus-scented.

Pelargonium crispum
Half-hardy evergreen perennial. Ht and spread 3 60cm (12-24in). Small pin flowers in summer. Small lobed leaves, green, crispy crinkled and lemon scente Neat habit.

Pelargonium crispum Crea 'Peach'
Half-hardy evergreen perennial. Ht and spread 3 60cm (12-24in). Small pin flowers in summer. Small lobed leaves, green with cream and yellow variegation, crispy crinkle and peach-scented.

A variety of scented geraniums

Pelargonium crispum 'Variegatum'

Half-hardy evergreen perennial. Ht and spread 30-60cm (12-24in). Small pink flowers in summer. Small 3-lobed leaves, green with cream variegation, crispy crinkled, and lemon scented.

Pelargonium denticulatum group

Half-hardy evergreen perennial. Ht and spread 1m (3ft). Small pinky-mauve flowers in summer. Deeply cut palmate leaves, green with a lemon scent.

Pelargonium denticulatum group 'Filicifolium'

Half-hardy evergreen perennial. Ht and spread 1m (3ft). Small pink flowers in summer. Very finely indented green leaves with a fine brown line running through, slightly sticky and not particularly aromatic, if anything a scent of balsam. Prone to white fly.

Pelargonium fragrans group

Half-hardy evergreen perennial. Ht and spread 30cm (12in). Small white flowers in summer. Greyish green leaves, rounded with shallow lobes, and a strong scent of nutmeg/pine.

Pelargonium fragrans group 'Fragrans variegatum'

Half-hardy evergreen perennial. Ht and spread 30cm (12in). Small white flowers in summer. Greyish green leaves with cream variegation, rounded with shallow lobes and a strong scent of nutmeg/pine.

Pelargonium 'Atomic Snowflake'

Pelargonium 'Lemon Fancy' in flower

Pelargonium graveolens
Rose Geranium

Half-hardy evergreen perennial. Ht 60cm-1m (24-36in). Spread up to 1m (3ft). Small pink flowers in summer. Fairly deeply cut green leaves with a rose/peppermint scent. One of the more hardy of this species, with good growth.

Pelargonium 'Lady Plymouth'

Half-hardy evergreen perennial. Ht and spread 30-60cm (12-24in) Small pink flowers in summer. Fairly deeply cut greyish green leaves with cream variegation and a rose/peppermint scent.

Pelargonium 'Lemon Fancy'

Half-hardy evergreen perennial. Ht 30-60cm (12-24in), spread 30-45cm (12-18in). Smallish pink flowers in summer. Small roundish green leaves with shallow lobes and an intense lemon scent.

Pelargonium 'Lilian Pottinger'

Half-hardy evergreen perennial. Ht 30-60cm (12-24in), spread 1m (3ft). Small whitish flowers in summer. Leaves brightish green, rounded, shallowly lobed with serrated edges. Soft to touch. Mild spicy apple scent.

Pelargonium 'Mabel Grey'

Half-hardy evergreen perennial. Ht 45-60cm (18-24in), spread 30-45cm (12-18in). Mauve flowers with deeper veining in summer. If I have a favourite, this is it: the leaves are diamond shaped, roughly textured, mid- green and oily when rubbed and very strongly lemon-scented.

Pelargonium odoratissimum

Half-hardy evergreen perennial. Ht 30-60cm (12-24in) spread 1m (3ft). Small white flowers in summer. Green, rounded, shallowly lobed leaves, fairly bright green in colour and soft to touch, with an apple scent. Trailing habit, looks good in large containers.

Pelargonium 'Prince of Orange'

Half-hardy evergreen perennial. Ht and spread 30-60cm (12-24in). Pretty pink/white flowers in summer. Green, slightly crinkled, slightly lobed leaves, with a refreshing orange scent. Prone to rust.

Pelargonium quercifolium
Oak-Leafed Pelargonium

Half-hardy evergreen perennial. Ht and spread up to 1m (3ft). Pretty pink/purple flowers in summer. Leaves oak-shaped, dark green with brown variegation, and slightly sticky. A different, spicy scent.

Pelargonium 'Royal Oak'

Half-hardy evergreen perennial. Ht 38cm (15in) spread 30cm (12in). Small pink/purple flowers in summer. Oak-shaped, dark green leaves with brown variegation, slightly sticky with spicy scent. Very similar to **P. quercifolium**, but with a more compact habit.

Pelargonium 'Rober's Lemon Rose'

Half-hardy evergreen perennial. Ht and spread up to 1m (3ft.). Pink flowers in summer. Leaves greyish green – oddly shaped, lobed and cut – with a rose scent. A fast grower, so pinch out the growing tips to maintain shape.

Oak-Leafed Pelargonium
Pelargonium quercifolium

Pelargonium tomentosum

Half-hardy evergreen perennial. Ht 30-60cm (12-24in), spread 1m (3ft). Small white flowers in summer. Large rounded leaves, shallow lobed, velvet grey-green in colour with a strong peppermint scent. Fast grower, so pinch out growing tips to maintain shape. Protect from full sun.

Pelargonium 'Chocolate Peppermint'

Pelargonium 'Attar of Roses'

CULTIVATION

Propagation
Seed
Although I have known scented geraniums to have been grown from seed, I do not recommend this method. Cuttings are much more reliable for the majority. However, if you want to have a go, sow in spring in a peat and grit compost at a temperature no lower than 15°C (59°F).

Cuttings
All scented geraniums can be propagated by softwood cuttings which generally take very easily in the summer. Take cutting about 10-15cm (4-6in) long and strip the leaves from the lower part with a sharp knife. At all costs do not tear the leaves

off as this will cause a hole in the stem and the cutting will be susceptible to disease, such as black leg. This is a major caveat for such as **Pelargonium crispum 'Variegatum'**. Use a sharp knife and slice the leaf off, insert the cutting into a tray containing equal parts bark and peat. Water in and put the tray away from direct sunlight. Keep an eye on the compost, making sure it does not thoroughly dry out, but only water if absolutely necessary. The cuttings should root in 2 to 3 weeks. Pot up into separate pots containing the bark, peat, grit mix of compost. Place in a cool greenhouse or cool conservatory for the winter, keeping the compost dry and watering only very occasionally. In the spring re-pot into larger pots and water sparingly. When they start to produce flower buds give them a liquid feed. In early summer pinch out the top growing points to encourage bushy growth.

Pests and Diseases
Unfortunately pelargoniums do suffer from a few diseases.

1 Cuttings can be destroyed by blackleg virus. The cutting turns black and falls over. The main cause of this is too much water. So keep the cuttings as dry as possible after the initial watering.

2 Grey mould (botrytis) is also caused by the plants being too wet and the air too moist. Remove damaged leaves carefully so as not to spread the disease, and burn. Allow the plants to dry out, and increase ventilation and spacing between plants.

3 Leaf gall appears as a mass of small proliferated shoots at the base of a cutting or plant. Destroy the plant, otherwise it could affect other plants.

4 Geraniums, like mint and comfrey, are prone to rust. Destroy the plant or it will spread to others.

5 Whitefly. Be vigilant. If you catch it early enough, you will be able to control it by spraying with a liquid horticultural soap. Follow manufacturer's instruction

Maintenance
Spring: Trim, slowly introduce watering, and sta feeding. Re-pot if necessary
Summer: Feed regularly. Trim to maintain shape.
Autumn: Take cuttings. Tri back plants. Bring in for th winter to protect from frost
Winter: Allow the plants to rest. Keep watering to a minimum.

Garden Cultivation
Scented pelargoniums are varied that they can look very effective grown in groups in the garden. Plan out as soon there is no danger of frost. Choose a warm site with well-drained soil. A good method is to sink the re-potted, over-wintered geraniums into th soil. This makes sure the initial compost is correct, and makes it easier to dig u the pot and bring inside before the first frost.

Harvest
Pick leaves during the growing season, for fresh u or for drying.
  Collect seeds before the seed pod ripens and ripen paper bags. If allowed to ripen on the plant, the pod will burst, scattering the seeds everywhere.

CONTAINER GROWING

Scented **pelargoniums** mak marvellous pot plants. They grow well, look good, and smell lovely. Pot up as described in Propagation. Place the containers so that you can rub the leaves as yo walk past.

CULINARY

Before artificial food flavourings were produced the Victorians used scented pelargonium leaves in the bottom of cake tins to flavour their sponges. Why not follow suit? When you grease and line the bottom of a 20cm (8in) sandwich tin, arrange approximately 20 leaves of either **'Lemon Fancy'**, **'Mabel Grey'**, or **'Graveolens'**. Fill the tin with a sponge mix of your choice and cook as normal. Remove the leaves with the lining paper when the cake has cooled. Scented pelargonium leaves add distinctive flavour to many dishes although, like bay leaves, they are hardly ever eaten, being removed after the cooking process. The main varieties used are **'Graveolens'**, **'Odoratissimum'**, **'Lemon Fancy'** and **'Attar of Roses'**.

Geranium Leaf Sorbet

Geranium Leaf Sorbet

12 scented Pelargonium graveolens leaves
75g/3oz/6 tablespoons caster sugar
300ml/½pint/1¼ cups water
Juice of 1 large lemon
1 egg white
4 leaves for decoration

Wash the leaves and shake them dry. Put the sugar and water in a saucepan and boil until the sugar has dissolved, stirring occasionally. Remove the pan from the heat. Put the 12 leaves in the pan with the sugar and water, cover and leave for 20 minutes. Taste. If you want a stronger flavour bring the liquid to the boil again add some fresh leaves and leave for a further 10 minutes. When you have the right flavour, strain the syrup into a rigid container, add the lemon juice and leave to cool. Place in the freezer until semi-frozen (approximately 45 minutes) – it must be firm, not mushy – and fold in the beaten egg white. Put back into freezer for a further 45 minutes. Scoop into individual glass bowls, and decorate with a geranium leaf.

Rose Geranium Punch

1.2 litre/2pints/5 cups of apple juice
4 limes
250g/8oz/1 cup sugar
6 leaves of graveolens
6 drops of green vegetable colouring (optional)

Boil the apple juice and sugar and geranium leaves for 5 minutes. Strain the liquid. Cool and add colouring if required. Thinly slice and crush limes, add to the liquid. Pour onto ice in glasses and garnish with geranium leaves.

Graveolens Geranium Butter

Butter pounded with the leaves makes a delicious filling for cakes and sweet biscuits. Spread on bread and top with apple jelly.

Rose Geranium Punch

OTHER USES

In Aromatherapy, Geranium oil is relaxing but use it in small quantities. Dilute 2 drops in 2 teaspoons of soy oil for a good massage, or to relieve pre-menstrual tension, dermatitis, eczema, herpes or dry skin.

WARNING

None of the **crispums** should be used in cooking as it is believed that they can upset the stomach.

Primula vulgaris

PRIMROSE

***Also known as Early Rose, Easter Rose, First Rose and May-Flooer.
From the family Primulaceae.***

Primula vulgaris
Primrose
Hardy perennial. Ht and spread 15cm (6in). The fresh yellow, sweetly scented flowers with darker yellow centres are borne singly on hairy stems in early spring. Leaves are mid-green and wrinkled.

This herald of spring is a native of Europe.
The name Primrose originates from the old Latin 'prima', meaning first, and 'rosa', meaning rose.

The polyanthus, which has been known in gardens since the 17th century, probably originates from crosses between coloured forms of the Primrose and the Cowslip.

In the Middle Ages concoctions were made from primroses which were used as a remedy for gout and rheumatism. The flowers were used in the preparation of love potions. An infusion of the roots was taken for nervous headaches.

The plant has become increasingly rare, in part due to the changing countryside. Legislation makes it illegal now to pick or dig up any wild plant and, with more sympathetic farming practices, one can see these plants beginning to re-establish in the hedgerows.

Primrose *Primula vulgaris*

CULTIVATION

Propagation
Seed
In summer sow the fresh seed when it is still slightly green and before it turns darkish brown and becomes dry. Sow in a prepared seed or plug tray and cover with Perlite. These fresh seeds usually germinate in a few weeks. Either winter in the plug trays, or prick out from seed trays when the seedlings are large enough and winter in pots for planting out into a prepared site the following spring.

The seed that one gets in seed packets should be sown in the autumn or early winter. Do not sow it directly into the ground where it can easily be lost. Water the seeds in; do not cover with compost, but cover with glass or polythene. To help the seeds germinate, leave the trays outside for the winter so that the seeds get the frost (stratification). Sometimes they take 2 years to germinate from the dry state, so leave the seed trays until the following year if nothing appears in the spring, checking the compost occasionally to make sure it does not dry out. When the seedlings are large enough, plant out in a prepared site in the garden 15cm (6in) apart.

Division
Established clumps (from your own or friends' gardens, not from the wild) can be divided very easily in the autumn.

Pests and Diseases
The only major pest to attack the primrose is the

imrose *Primula vulgaris*

Some **Primula** species can cause a form of contact dermatitis, characterized by a violent vascular eruption in the fingers and forearms. Hyper-sensitive individuals should avoid these plants.

Primrose tisane

MEDICINAL

Its medicinal use is really in the past, though it is still used occasionally as an expectorant for the treatment of bronchitis. A tisane, which is a mild sedative and good for anxiety and insomnia, can be made from the leaves and flowers.

Primrose salad

CULINARY

The flowers are lovely in green salads, and they can be crystallized to decorate puddings and cakes.
The young leaves make an interesting vegetable if steamed and tossed in butter.

ne weevil. Pollinated rimrose flowers produce icky seeds that attract ants; ey then disperse them round the garden, which is hy you sometimes see lants where you least xpect them.

Maintenance
pring: Plant out young lants.
ummer: Sow fresh seed.
utumn: Divide established lants.
Vinter: Sow dry seed that eeds stratification. No need o protect plants, fully hardy.

Garden Cultivation
Vhen planting primroses ear in mind that their atural habitat is in edgerows and under eciduous trees and that herefore they prefer a moist oil, and will tolerate heavy oils, in semi-shade. Planted n a very well-sheltered site, hey often open early in pring.
If you are growing rimroses in a wild garden

make sure you do not cut the grass until mid-summer when the plants will have seeded themselves.

Harvest
Pick flowers for fresh use any time. Pick young leaves to use fresh. In summer collect seed for immediate sowing.

CONTAINER GROWING

Primroses can be grown in containers and look very attractive and heartening especially if spring is damp and miserable. Use a soil-based compost. Keep the plant well watered and feed only occasionally with liquid fertilizer, once in the spring after flowering is sufficient. This is primarily a wild plant and does not benefit from over feeding.

Thymus

THYME

From the family Labiatae.

This is a genus comprising numerous species that are very diverse in appearance and come from many different parts of the world. They are found as far afield as Greenland and Western Asia, although the majority grow in the Mediterranean region.

This ancient herb was used by the Egyptians in oil form for embalming. The Greeks used it in their baths and as an incense in their temples. The Romans used it to purify their rooms, and most probably its use spread through Europe as their invasion train swept as far as Britain. In the Middle Ages drinking it was part of a ritual to enable one to see fairies, and it was one of many herbs used in nosegays to purify the odours of disease. Owing to its antiseptic properties, judges also used it along with rosemary to prevent goal fever.

Common Thyme
Thymus vulgaris

Silver Posie Thyme
Thymus vulgaris 'Silver Posie'

SPECIES

There are so many species of Thyme that I am only going to mention a few of interest. New ones are being discovered each year. They are eminently collectable. Unfortunately their names can be unreliable, a nursery preferring its pet name or one traditional to it, rather than the correct one.

Thymus caespititius (Thymus azoricus)
Caespititius Thyme
Evergreen hardy perennial. Ht 10cm (4in), spread 20cm (8in). Pale pink flowers in summer. The leaves narrow, bright green and close together on the stem. Makes an attractive low growing mound, good between paving stones.

Thymus camphoratus
Camphor Thyme
Evergreen half-hardy perennial. Ht 30cm (12in), spread 20cm (8in). Pink/mauve flowers in summer, large green leaves smelling of camphor. Makes a beautiful compact bush.

Thymus cilicicus
Cilicicus Thyme
Evergreen hardy perennial. Ht 5cm (2in), spread 20cm (8in). Pink flowers in summer. The leaves are bright green, narrow and pointed, growing close together on the stem with an odd celery scent. Makes an attractive low growing mound, good between paving stones.

Thymus x citriodorus
Lemon Thyme
Evergreen hardy perennial. Ht 30 cm (12in), spread 20cm (8in). Pink flowers in summer. Fairly large green leaves with a strong lemon scent. Excellent culinary thyme, combines well with many chicken or fish dishes.

Wild Creeping Thyme
Thymus Praecox spp. arcticus

Thymus x citriodorus 'Archer's Gold'
Archer's Gold Thyme
Evergreen hardy perennial Ht 10cm (4in), spread 20c (8in). Pink/mauve flower in summer. A mound of green/gold leaves. Decorative and culinary, i has a mild thyme flavour.

Thymus x citriodorus 'Bertram Anderson'
Bertram Anderson Thyme
Evergreen hardy perennial Ht 10cm (4in), spread 20c (8in). Pink/mauve flower in summer . More of a round mound than Archer Gold and the leaves are slightly rounder with a mo even golden look to the leaves. Decorative and culinary, it has a mild thyn flavour.

Thymus x citriodorus 'Fragrantissimus'
Orange Scented Thyme
Evergreen hardy perennial Ht 30 cm (12in), spread 20cm (8in). Small pale pink/white flowers in summer. The leaves are small, narrow, greyish gree and smell of spicy orange Combines well with stir fr dishes, poultry – especiall duck, and even treacle pudding.

Thymus x citriodorus 'Golden King'
Golden King Thyme
Evergreen hardy perennia Ht 30cm (12in) spread 20c (8in). Pink flowers in the summer. Fairly large gree leaves variegated with gol strongly lemon scented. Excellent culinary thyme combines well with many dishes, like chicken, fish a salad dressing.

Thymus x citriodorus 'Silver Queen'

Silver Queen Thyme
vergreen hardy perennial.
Ht 30cm (12in) spread
0cm (8in). Pink flowers in
the summer. Fairly large
leaves, grey with silver
ariegation, a strong lemon
scent. Excellent culinary
hyme, combines well with
nany dishes, like chicken,
fish and salad dressing.

Thymus doerfleri

Doerfleri Thyme
Evergreen half-hardy
perennial. Ht 2cm (1in),
pread 20cm (8in). Mauve
pink flowers in summer,
grey, hairy, thin leaves,
which are mat forming.
ecorative thyme, good for
ckeries, hates being wet in
inter. Originates from the
Balkan Peninsula.

Thymus doerfleri 'Bressingham Pink'

Bressingham Pink Thyme
vergreen hardy perennial.
It 2cm (1in), spread 20cm
8in). Mauve/pink flowers
in summer. Thin, green,
airy leaves, which are mat
orming. Decorative thyme,
good for rockeries, hates
being wet in winter.

Thymus 'Doone Valley'

Doone Valley Thyme
vergreen hardy perennial.
It 8cm (3in), spread 20cm
(8in). Purple flowers in
ummer. Round variegated
reen and gold leaves with a
lemon scent. Very
ecorative, can be used in
cooking if nothing else is
available.

Thymus herba-barona

Caraway Thyme
Evergreen hardy perennial.
Ht 2cm (1in), spread 20cm
(8in). Rose coloured flowers
in summer. Dark green
small leaves with a unique
caraway scent. Good in
culinary dishes especially stir
fry and meat. It combines
well with beef.

Thymus praecox spp. arcticus

Wild Creeping Thyme
Also known as Mother of
Thyme and Creeping
Thyme.
Evergreen hardy perennial.
Ht 2cm (1in), spread 20cm
(8in). Pale mauve flowers in
summer. Small dark green
leaves which, although
mildly scented, can be used
in cooking. Wild thyme has
been valued by herbalists for
many centuries.

Thymus praecox 'Porlock'

Porlock Thyme
Evergreen hardy perennial.
Ht 30cm (12in), spread
20cm (8in). Pink flowers in
summer. Fairly large green
leaves with a mild but
definite thyme flavour and
scent. Excellent culinary
thyme. Medicinal properties
are anti-bacterial and anti-
fungal.

Thymus pseudolanuginosus

Woolly Thyme
Evergreen hardy perennial.
Ht 2cm (1in), spread 20cm
(8in). Pale pink/mauve
flowers for most of the
summer. Grey hairy mat-
forming leaves. Good for
rockeries and in stone paths
or walls. Dislikes wet winters.

Thymus pulegioïdes

Broad Leaved Thyme
Evergreen hardy perennial.
Ht 8cm (3in), spread 20cm
(8in). Pink/mauve flowers
in summer. Large round
dark green leaves with a
strong thyme flavour. Good
for culinary uses, excellent
for ground cover and good
in hanging baskets.

Lemon Thyme

Thymus x citriodorus

Thymus richardii spp. nitidus 'Peter Davis'

Peter Davis Thyme
Evergreen hardy perennial.
Ht 8cm (3in), spread 20cm
(8in). Attractive pink/
mauve flowers in summer.
Thin grey/green leaves,
mild scent. Very attractive
thyme, good in rockeries or
formal herb gardens.

Thymus serpyllum albus

White Thyme
Evergreen hardy perennial,
prostrate form, a creeper.
White flowers in summer.
Bright green small leaves.
Decorative aromatic and
good ground cover.

Thymus serpyllum 'Annie Hall'

Annie Hall Thyme
Evergreen hardy perennial,
prostrate form, a creeper.
Pale pink flowers in
summer. Small green leaves.
Decorative, aromatic and
good ground cover.

Pink Chintz Thyme

Thymus serpyllum 'Pink Chintz'

Thymus serpyllum coccineus

Coccineus Thyme
Also known as Creeping Red
Thyme.
Evergreen hardy perennial,
prostrate form, a creeper.
Red flowers in summer.
Green small leaves.
Decorative, aromatic and
good ground cover.

Thymus serpyllum 'Goldstream'

Goldstream Thyme
Evergreen hardy perennial,
prostrate form, a creeper.
Pink/mauve flowers in
summer. Green/gold
variegated small leaves.
Decorative, aromatic and
good ground cover.

Goldstream Thyme

Thymus serpyllum 'Goldstream'

Thymus serpyllum 'Lemon Curd'

Lemon Curd Thyme
Evergreen hardy perennial,
prostrate form, a creeper.
White/pink flowers in
summer. Bright green
lemon scented small leaves.
Decorative, aromatic and
good ground cover. Can be
used in cooking if nothing
else available.

Thymus serpyllum 'Minimus'

Minimus Thyme
Evergreen hardy perennial,
prostrate form, a creeper.
Pink flowers in summer.
Tiny leaves, very compact.
Decorative, aromatic and
good ground cover. The
leaves grow so close together
that it is ideal for growing
between pavings and
alongside paths.

Thymus serpyllum 'Pink Chintz'

Pink Chintz Thyme
Evergreen hardy perennial,
prostrate form, a creeper.
Pale pink flowers in
summer. Grey green small
hairy leaves. Decorative,
aromatic and good ground
cover. Does not particularly
like being wet in winter.

Thymus serpyllum 'Rainbow Falls'

Rainbow Falls Thyme
Evergreen hardy perennial,
prostrate form, a creeper.
Purple flowers in summer.
Variegated green/gold small
leaves. Decorative, aromatic
and good ground cover.

Thymus serpyllum 'Russetings'

Russetings Thyme
Evergreen hardy perennial,
prostrate form, a creeper.
Purple/mauve flowers in
summer. Small green leaves.
Decorative, aromatic and
good ground cover.

Thymus serpyllum 'Snowdrift'
Snowdrift Thyme
Evergreen hardy perennial, prostrate form, a creeper. Masses of white flowers in summer. Small green round leaves. Decorative, aromatic and good ground cover.

Thymus vulgaris
Common (Garden) Thyme
Evergreen hardy perennial. Ht 30cm (12in), spread 20cm (8in). Mauve flowers in summer. Thin green aromatic leaves. This is the thyme everyone knows. Use in stews, salads, sauces etc. Medicinal properties are anti-bacterial and anti-fungal.

Thymus vulgaris aureus
Golden Thyme
Evergreen hardy perennial. Ht 30cm (12in), spread 20cm (8in). Pale pink /lilac flowers. Green leaves that turn gold in summer, they have a good flavour and combine well with vegetarian dishes.

Thymus vulgaris 'Lucy'
Lucy Thyme
Evergreen hardy perennial. Ht 30cm (12in), spread 20cm (8in). The thyme sometimes does not flower, and if it does, it is a very pale pink flower and not very prolific. The leaves are very small green. Excellent culinary thyme. Medicinal properties are anti-bacterial and anti-fungal.

Coccineus Thyme
Thymus serpyllum Coccineus **and Snowdrift Thyme**
Thymus serpyllum 'Snowdrift'

Thymus vulgaris 'Silver Posie'
Silver Posie Thyme
Evergreen hardy perennial. Ht 30cm (12in), spread 20cm (8in). Pale pink/lilac flower. The leaves have a very pretty grey/silver variegation with a tinge of pink on the under-side. This is a good culinary thyme and looks very attractive in salads.

Thymus zygis
Zygis Thyme
Evergreen half-hardy perennial. Ht 30cm (12in), spread 20cm (8in). White attractive flowers. Small thin grey/green leaves which are aromatic. This is an attractive thyme which is good for rockeries. Originates from Spain and Portugal, therefore does not like cold wet winters.

Upright Thymes
Up to 30cm (12in): Caespititius, Archers Gold, Bertram Anderson, Peter Davis.

30cm (12in) and above: Camphor, Lucy, Lemon, Orange Scented, Golden King, Porlock, Common (Garden), Golden, Silver Posie, Zygis.

Creeping Thymes
Cilicicus, Doerfleri, Bressingham Pink, Doone Valley, Wild Creeping, Woolly, Broad Leaved, White, Annie Hall, Coccineus, Gold Stream, Lemon Curd, Minimus, Pink Chintz, Rainbow Falls, Russetings, Snowdrift.

CULTIVATION

Propagation
To maintain the true plant, it is better to grow the majority of thymes from softwood cuttings. Only a very few, such as common and wild creeping thyme, can be propagated successfully from seed.

Seed
Sow the very fine seed in early spring using the cardboard technique on the surface of prepared trays (seed or plug), using the bark, peat, grit compost and a bottom heat of 15-21°C (60-70°F). Do not cover. Keep watering to the absolute minimum, as these seedlings are prone to damping off disease. When the young plants are large enough and after a period of hardening off, plant out in the garden in late spring/ early summer, 23-38cm (9-15in) apart.

Cuttings
Thymes are easily increased by softwood cuttings from new growth in early spring or summer. The length of the cutting should be 5-8cm (2-3in). Use the bark, peat, grit mix of compost. Winter the young plants under protection and plant out the following spring.

Division
Creeping thymes put out aerial roots as they spread, which make them very easy to divide.

Silver Posie Thyme
Thymus vulgaris 'Silver Posie'

Layering
An ideal method for mature thymes that are getting a bit woody. Use either the strong branch method of layering in early autumn or mound layer in early spring.

Pests and Diseases
Being such an aromatic plant it does not normally suffer from pests but, if the soil or compost is too rich, thyme may be attacked by aphids. Treat with a liquid horticultural soap. All varieties will rot off if they become too wet in a cold winter.

Maintenance
Spring: Sow seeds. Trim old plants. Layer old plants.
Summer: Take cuttings of non-flowering shoots. Trim back after flowering.
Autumn: Protect tender thymes.
Winter: Protect containers and only water if absolutely necessary.

Garden Cultivation
Thymes need to be grown in poor soil, in a well-drained bed to give their best flavour. They are drought-loving plants and will need protection from cold winds, hard and wet winters. Sow seed when the soil has warmed and there is no threat of frost. Thin on average to 20cm (8in) apart.
It is essential to trim all thymes after flowering; this not only promotes new growth, but also stops the plant becoming woody and sprawling in the wrong direction.
In very cold areas grow it in the garden as an annual or in containers and then winter with protection.

Harvest
As thyme is an evergreen it can be picked fresh all year round provided you are not too greedy. For preserving, pick before it is in flower. Either dry the leaves or put them in a vinegar or oil.